BLOOD SUGAR

BLOOD SUGAR

INSPIRING RECIPES

FOR ANYONE FACING THE CHALLENGE
OF DIABETES AND MAINTAINING GOOD HEALTH

Michael Moore

NEW
HOLLAND

INSIDE

For my wonderful friends and family.

FOREWORD

I have known Michael for years and we have crossed paths many times in our careers. I have seen him take on big challenges in his professional life—owning and operating top restaurants both in London and Sydney. He is highly respected by many chefs across the globe.

When I heard about his recent health challenges it certainly shook me up, and it was felt throughout our circle of chefs.

How could this happen to a fit, active and healthy man?

In this book, Michael opens up and talks candidly about his biggest life challenge—dealing with diabetes and surviving a massive stroke.

Michael is a huge inspiration to anyone dealing with a chronic illness. He's a living breathing example of someone who has faced his illness head on, always looking ahead. His endless positivity, motivation and drive is what helped him survive.

With his extensive background and understanding of ingredients and cooking techniques, Michael has created a collection of fantastic recipes that capture the freshness and lightness of great healthy food with a restaurant-quality edge.

There can often be a disparity between restaurant-quality food and diet food, but with Michael's skills as a professional chef and his experience as a diabetic, this book bridges this gap and places it firmly at the quality end of cooking.

To my knowledge, Michael is the first high profile chef to write a book from this unique viewpoint.

Blood Sugar has recipes that everyone can enjoy, with simple explanations that will empower any home cook to create inspiring, tasty, healthy meals.

Curtis Stone

MY STORY

Through my whole life I have had a fire burning inside me, producing seemingly endless amounts of energy and positive drive, resulting in a fearless confidence, which constantly pushes me to chase my (sometimes) wild dreams and to achieve the best results I can.

From a very young age I could cook. It came to me naturally. I thrived on stress and achievement. So when it came to choosing a career, I naturally chose one that was a 'pressure cooker', a dynamic growing industry where I could be creative. I chose to be a chef. I loved the daily challenge of a kitchen, the preparation and then the madness of a service.

Long hours, tough conditions and adversity—it was all part of the game and a large part of why I chose this industry. Going to work in the morning and putting on boots that were still soggy with sweat from the night before meant that I had worked hard; it was all part of the quest to push myself to the limit.

As a chef, I never really felt like I was going to work. I was a lucky man, living my life doing what I loved to do. I still feel the same way and I often meet people in other professions who feel like me. They are nearly always in creative industries—art, music, food and design. I would love my kids to find this joy in their lives as they grow.

'Rise to the challenge and beat the odds, the competition is standing next to you.' This was my mantra, and I hoped it was going to help me fulfil my dreams.

I had been thinking like this every day from the age of 15. Then at 35 I was diagnosed with diabetes.

My doctor said I was the most unusual person to become a diabetic. I was very fit, active and healthy; I never smoked nor was I a big drinker. I had always looked after myself, even while I worked long hours in an industry full of vices like alcohol, drugs and cigarettes. In fact, sometimes the only way to get a break during the day was to go for a 'smoke'—even if you didn't!

I had just opened our new restaurant and my wife Angela had given birth to our first child, Eloise. I had been working night and day. I was feeling tired and run down, with an unusual thirst I just couldn't satisfy. I drank about 10 bottles of lemon cordial in one night and ate a massive packet of jellybeans in one go. My body kept craving for more sugar as the days went on. I realised something was wrong and when my doctor tested me the next day, my blood sugar reading was 29 (normal is about 4).

I was sent to the endocrinologist and officially diagnosed diabetic. I may even have had it my whole life. This came as a great shock.

I felt my life was in good order at that time. What could I possibly change to cope with this new diagnosis? For the first year or two it didn't seem so hard. I was just taking a couple of pills a day, increasing my exercise and laying off the sweet things. I was probably in denial, thinking it would just go away. Gradually my visits to the endocrinologist became further apart and less important. I was feeling fine and continued to pursue my very busy life.

I have since learnt this was a big mistake! Gradually my drug regime changed as the degeneration took effect and I became insulin dependent. I was still unaware of the serious health risks that diabetes carried.

Fast-forward eight years. One lazy Sunday I was out to dinner with my family. I remember it all so clearly. It felt like I'd been hit by a truck. One minute I was standing at the barbecue, the next minute I hit the floor. My wife Angela was with me, and at first she thought I was having a diabetic hypo and called an ambulance immediately. She realised it was more serious when I wasn't able to drink the lemonade to bring my sugars back up because my face was paralysed down one side. She looked me in the eyes and said 'I think you've had a stroke, there's an ambulance coming'. My kids witnessed the whole thing and it took a while for Eloise, my daughter, to get the vision out of her head. It was a very confronting thing for a family to experience. Angela's quick thinking saved my life.

From this day, my life changed forever.

If you have a stroke you can take great comfort in knowing that the doctors are very systematic and will test you for everything. Even the cleaner at the hospital knew what test I would be having next!

'Had a stroke? Yeah, they'll give you a blood-thinning booster, do an MRI scan, do a million tests and send you on your way in 10 days or so.'

I was really scared for the first time in my life, I began to read and study what was going on. Some of the facts were really confronting. Why did this happen to me? There is no clear answer. There is a link to diabetes, but in my case there is still no firm conclusion as to why I had the stroke. I was told the chances of another stroke occurring within days after the initial one was quite high.

So I lay in hospital hoping that my body would not suffer another stroke. It was like waiting for the ball to drop into place on the roulette wheel; it seemed to spin forever.

If someone had said to me at this point, "Give me everything you own and I'll guarantee that you can walk along the beach at the weekend with your wife and kids" I'd have taken the deal. Luckily I did manage to walk along the beach with my family on the day I was discharged from hospital. It was the best day of my life!

In the weeks before the stroke I felt super fit—riding my bike, running, going to the gym. I just remember feeling great and strong.

However, while at the gym a week before it happened, the floor did go soft and feel spongy under my feet and my legs gave way. I didn't fall over but it was a strange feeling. Maybe this was a small warning but who knows? If you have experienced anything like this, go to your doctor—I wish I had.

All the professionals gave me hope and confidence that a positive outcome was possible. While I did cry a lot at this time, they all helped to support me.

The stroke was caused by a large blood clot that ran up my neck, through the clear veins of a fit young man. It fired into my brain and fortunately landed in a place where it did not cause too much damage. I feel like the luckiest man to be alive.

Obviously I had to rethink all of the food that I had been eating to manage diabetes and keep my health on track, but was determined to continue eating quality food, so decided to write this book, to provide some light into the 'gastronomic wilderness' of diet food.

I have not written a 'diet book'. This is a collection of recipes I have developed over time to help keep me on track and still enjoy sensational food.

So if you have diabetes, or have had a stroke, or if you just want to eat good food while looking after your health, these recipes are for you.

You can enjoy great food and good times with friends and family over delicious healthy food.

I hope this book brings some joy to you or someone you love.

Michael Moore

TIME FOR CHANGE!

I love great food—I love cooking it and I love eating it. All types of food—Asian, Japanese, French, Italian. You name it.

When I was diagnosed as diabetic, and particularly after my stroke, I had to change the way I thought about the food I was eating. I've continued to experiment and celebrate food in my restaurants and cafes, but I had to have a really, really close look at everything I was eating, all the time, and listen to my body.

I am a very busy person. My life has not slowed down! So I struggled to think of food in a simple way that I could use each day. The answer came in one word: Fuel. I could have easily called this book Fuel, but I chose Blood Sugar because that is what the Fuel affects.

I realised three things that made a lot of sense to me, that help me to understand the way my body uses fuel. It's simple. I look at everything I am going to eat and break it down into three easy-to-understand headings—Fire, Coal and Water. I look at each and every plate, dish or snack I am going to eat and ask myself what category is this in? It works for me and may well help you understand what you are eating.

'FIRE, WATER AND COAL FOOD'

Imagine that you are a steam engine and that your stomach is a fire that needs to burn to produce energy. It needs to be on all the time and to burn evenly and slowly. What are you going to throw into it? If you put coal or a log on the fire it will burn for hours. If you throw petrol onto the fire you get a big flash of flame and explosion of high heat and it's gone. You need to add water to calm it down.

The way I think about food roughly corresponds to the Glycemic Index. The Glycemic Index or GI describes carbohydrates according to their effect on our blood sugar (or glucose) levels. Low GI foods have the least effect on blood sugar and are the secret to long-term health. High GI foods cause a rapid rise in blood sugar.

Fire foods have a high GI—above 70. Fire foods are like throwing gasoline onto a fire—they explode with no benefit.

Water foods have a low GI—below 55. Water foods are fresh and have smaller effects on blood sugar levels.

Coal foods also have a low GI—they are the real fuel, and give you a long slow burn with warm embers.

This general way of grouping food helps me in my daily life. It's certainly not meant to be used as a medical system—I still monitor medically my sugar levels and other indicators. I also look closely at the GI Index in more detail. If you are a diabetic, your health professionals will advise you about your lifestyle. Always consult them about your diet and nutrition.

FIRE FOOD

Foods I call 'Fire Foods' are the hardest to resist and are often the most tempting to snack on! They are highly processed starchy, fatty or sugary foods and always have a high GI. They all give you an instant spike in blood sugar levels but offer little or no energy benefits to your body. For diabetics, they are definitely the devil in disguise. The flames are impressive but it is all show and no go.

Foods that fall into this category are highly processed, low in fibre and low in protein. They are easily converted by your body from starch into glucose, which is then absorbed into your blood and it is this that makes your blood sugars spike. They are foods above 70 GI. The foods I look at with caution in this group may surprise you.

Rice, pasta and white bread: Starch is easily converted into glucose by your body, so these foods should be avoided as much as possible. Instant white rice, short grain rice, jasmine and risotto rice are all bad for diabetics. Rice crackers may seem to be a healthy option, but they have a high GI. Highly processed white bread, Turkish bread, English muffins and pancakes are off the menu, as are Danish pastries and croissants. They are full of fat and are made with white flour and are often combined with a sugar and fruit topping. I love pasta—so I always eat small portions of artisan pasta made with durum wheat or semolina flour.

Potatoes without their skin unfortunately are high in starch and are really off my menu. I know I have eaten my last fried potato chip and comforting bowl of creamy mashed potato! I am lucky I have never really enjoyed white bread, so I don't miss it at all! I now enjoy heavily seeded bread if possible handmade by a quality baker rather than a factory. Making your own bread is also a good option—you may add seeds or bran or wheat germ, all of which will improve the eating quality for your body.

Sweet things are obviously 'fire food'. I avoid sugar, sweet chocolate or confectionary. It is a discipline you need to have. Biscuits are loaded with sugar, and the ones you have with cheese are also often high in salt and fat. Jellies and boiled sweets, cakes, muffins and cordial drinks are very high in sugar.

Many fruits and fruit juices have a high level of sugar. Due to the process of squeezing fresh fruit juice, almost all of the fibre is removed which leaves a sugar-based liquid that is often no better for you than soft drink. I often freeze fresh fruit juice and mix it into a glass of cold water, this can satisfy my craving for juice. You can mix fruit and vegetable juice together; the addition of fresh carrot or celery dilutes the overall sugar content and increases the volume of the drink. Watermelons, dates, mangoes, pineapples, raisins—all these fruits have high GI. Check the sugar content of the fruit you are regularly eating and you will be surprised.

All of my recipes in Blood Sugar use minimum 'fire foods'.

My main artillery against 'fire foods' is agave syrup which I use in most of my recipes. Agave nectar and syrup is produced from the Agave plant which originates in South America. Low glycemic index agave is absorbed slowly into the bloodstream and is a diabetic friendly sugar substitute. It's readily available in delicatessens, health food stores and supermarkets.

WATER FOOD

Let it rain, let it rain, let it rain! What I call 'Water Foods' keep you hydrated, feeling full and well. Mostly crisp crunchy and delicious, this is the food group that can satisfy your hunger with minimal penalty.

Foods in this category are vegetables. They are mostly grown above the ground and have absorbed a lot of water during their lifetime. They exclude starchy potatoes, pumpkin and parsnips

The water-based vegetables are lettuce, cucumber, green beans, tomatoes, all fresh herbs, carrots—basically what you find at the fresh fruit and veg market. Some foods, like artichokes and asparagus, are even better because of their high fibre content.

'Water foods' have minimal effect on blood sugar, and I try and eat as much of these as possible. My rule is that if it's crisp, fresh and crunchy I can have as much as I like—either raw or cooked.

When I cook, I am always looking for freshness and flavour. Great vegetables are best drizzled with a little olive oil, salt and pepper and some chopped fresh herbs.

These foods will aid hydration and are also easy to grow yourself. They will also be the cheapest foods in the shops so they are ideal on a number of levels!

Some easy recipes for water foods involve herbs and spices. Some spices also stimulate metabolism and have other health benefits.

The foods in this group are led by the hero, the tomato. These are easily the most versatile of the water foods and they underpin all of the Mediterranean cuisines such as Spanish, Italian, Greek, Turkish and French. A ripe tomato simply sliced with some fresh ground black pepper and a pinch of sea salt with ripped basil is a great side dish or salad. Learn to cook with tomatoes! They are really good for you!

The humble bean is also a lead player in the Water Foods. Green beans, Roman beans and borlotti beans are ideal for salads or served hot with a little fresh chilli, garlic and lemon. Ripped marjoram or lemon thyme work well with these beans.

Cucumber and salad leaves are fantastic with some fresh chopped parsley and mint. Add a spoon of natural yoghurt and serve with grilled fish or chicken. Even when you are buying these, you start to feel healthy! I like to dip romaine lettuce leaves in natural yoghurt and fresh black pepper as a snack while I am waiting for dinner to cook.

Broccoli, broccolini, cauliflower and carrot are delicious and once again, good for salads or in pasta or as a side dish. I love salt and red chilli, with these vegetables. A simple drizzle of soy sauce can transform broccolini or broccoli. Add a small knob of butter to hot cauliflower and the taste is amazing.

Mushrooms and red capsicum (peppers) are fantastically high in vitamins, full of flavour and low GI. Why not make sauces with them or roast them and crumble fetta cheese over the top? Make a low GI soup or grill them on seeded toast for breakfast.

Some fruits are great 'water foods' and I use them in many recipes. Fruits that have the seeds or skin on become high-fibre alternatives. Strawberries, blueberries, passionfruit, figs with the skin on—you will find all these fruits in this book.

COAL FOOD

If it looks like it will be slow to break down, it will be 'Coal Food'. Learn to love the long, slow burn. If it's high protein, crunchy and high in fibre, it's coal food and it's energy sustaining. Learn to love your coal food and life will be better for you.

The harder your body needs to work to break food down, the better it is for you. This food group is the one that you need the most of to maintain a healthy blood sugar balance.

Coal foods are high in fibre and high in protein, give you sustained energy and stabilise your sugars. Coal foods will make you feel better for longer, helping keep everything steady and stable. They will sustain your energy and endurance. You will feel full by eating these foods and they will help you maintain regular weight and body fat levels.

Nuts and seeds are nature's own coal foods and they are always with me. Almonds are my favourite. They have a good protein level and have monounsaturated fats. There are many benefits in using nuts as your 'go to' snack. Try to avoid the higher fat content nuts such as macadamias and brazil nuts. Walnuts and pecans have a higher fibre content due to their skin, so I love to include these in salads and sauces. Pumpkin seeds and sunflower seeds are also great coal foods.

Fresh pesto with walnuts is healthy, easy to make and tastes great. Try to leave the walnuts more on the chunky side rather than grinding them to paste.

Coal foods are also protein foods. Protein takes a long time to break down in the body. You should try to eat a balance of fish and meat, taking care not to eat too much saturated fat. My recipes include trimmed meat and lean cuts—this doesn't make them less delicious!

If you do not eat meat you are going to have to work harder to get good protein in your diet. This can come from nuts, legumes and pulses, fish, cheese and tofu.

Lentils, chickpeas and many different beans all have a good protein level; however, they do have some carbohydrate. They are great for absorbing flavour and are low in fat. I like to combine these with 'water foods' and some spices to create tasty salads, soups and braised dishes that everyone loves. Tofu is easily available to buy as a protein supplement. It's great in soups, salads and dips. I also use it to boost smoothies and milk drinks, it has little flavour of its own and will adopt the flavour of the product you use it with.

Most diets advise you to limit your intake of diary, due to their saturated fat content. I use soft cheese like low-fat ricotta which has a good protein content. Natural unsweetened low-fat yoghurt and low-fat feta cheese are good high-protein choices.

I love egg whites! Egg yolks do have a high fat and cholesterol level. I use egg whites instead in scrambled eggs and omelettes.

Fresh fish is the best coal food. Omega 3 oils help maintain healthy blood density which is important for stroke or diabetic patients. Fresh salmon and ocean trout are great eaten raw, like sashimi. White fish like snapper or bass are easy and quick to cook, grilled with little or no oil. Shellfish needs to be eaten in moderation—prawns have an elevated cholesterol content, while scallops and crab are a healthy treat.

If it's white, sweet or deep-fried, there's a fair chance it's not good for you. If it's crunchy and high in fibre, it's energy sustaining.

BURN

Strong consistent exercise is best for everyone. We all need to consume the sugar in our blood. This can only be done by insulin or exercise.

This is the exercise part of the equation—after fire, water and coal comes the burn. You need to do steady exercise for a minimum of 20 minutes to see a reduction in blood sugar. It doesn't need to be intense, just a good steady walk, swim or cycle. If you can push yourself, go for it but talk to the doctor first.

Good eating and good cooking starts with good shopping. The enemy is highly processed food, full of sugar and carbohydrate. You can enjoy a small piece of chocolate or a sprinkle of sugar in your coffee but white rice and mashed potatoes are full of carbs and are off the menu.

You will need to get used to reading the labels on food and understanding how they affect your blood sugar. A balanced meal is best. The protein should be lean and when eaten together with a carbohydrate, the GI is lowered.

Remember your diet should still taste good but must be low GI, high protein, high fibre and full of complex carbs and vegetables. Fill your fridge full of vegetables and try to snack on them rather than biscuits or carb laden health bars.

DIET AND EXERCISE ARE SUPREMELY IMPORTANT

Here are some tips so you don't miss an opportunity to reduce sugars:

- Never stand on an escalator, take the stairs if you can

- Walk between jobs, meetings or even walk the kids to school

- Go as far away as you can to get your lunch—walk there and walk back again

- Playing a round of golf? Walk don't drive a buggy!

- Swimming is a great low-impact exercise and can be done, any day any time, why not join a squad?

- On the road or on the wind trainer I am sure I will live longer due to my push bike!

- Try to do something every day—even if it's small your fitness will grow.

You are on a diet, whether you like it or not. So watch what you eat!

Find something you love to do—cycle, dance, golf, swim run or walk.

MY TIPS ON BLOOD SUGAR

Here are a few tips that I use to manage my health:

SHOPPING

Good health, good eating and good cooking all start with good shopping! I always make a list and try to plan my meals ahead but I always leave a blank space on the shopping list for the seasonal and great ingredients I will see. At the fruit and veg market you will find mostly 'free food' so you can go a bit crazy. Be careful not to be tempted by the sweet treats. If you don't buy them and take them home you are far less likely to be tempted in the evening when you feel like a snack.

My main artillery against 'fire foods' is agave syrup which I use in most of my recipes. Agave nectar and syrup is produced from the Agave plant which originates in South America. Low glycemic index agave is absorbed slowly into the bloodstream and is a diabetic friendly sugar substitute. It's readily available in delicatessens, health food stores and supermarkets.

LABELS

Once you start reading the labels on prepared foods, you may be in for a shock when you see what's in them! You need to look at the total carbohydrate content as well as the sugars. One easy tip to remember is try to avoid anything with more than 10% sugar or 30% total carbohydrates.

PORTION CONTROL

When I was first diagnosed I couldn't believe how small a 'meal portion' really should be. In general, we all eat far too much. If you are overweight, just measure a portion out and try to adjust your consumption.

MEALS IN A DAY

I feel a lot better if I eat more small meals a day—usually up to six. They are all balanced with some protein and a small amount of carbs, this keeps my metabolism moving along and the sugars nice and steady. If you are going to eat a big meal or need a lot of energy, maybe you are going on a walk or playing golf, try to eat a big breakfast and gradually have smaller meals later in the day.

HYDRATION AND EXERCISE

Before I had my stroke, I was super fit and exercising a lot. I was always working out. I wonder now if I was often dehydrated. Being properly hydrated is paramount to good kidney function and keeping your blood thin. It is amazing how healthy you feel as well. Eating plenty of the water foods also helps.

WEIGHING IN

Very close to portion control is the correct weight of what you eat, so buy some good kitchen scales and monitor the portion sizes accurately. You can even record the macro nutrients daily to help weight control. Also try to maintain a good steady body weight and low body fat percentage.

REWARDING YOURSELF

Your diabetic diet never really leaves your mind so sometimes you have to cut yourself some slack. If you must have a treat like chocolate, make sure it is good quality, preferably dark chocolate (less sugar) and enjoy it slowly! I like to treat myself while I'm out walking or riding my bike. At least I am using the sugar up while I exercise. Try my Baked Orange and Peanut Delicious for a treat.

SUGAR HITS (MANAGING LOW SUGARS)

I love good quality, natural-fruit jellies! They are my weakness, so I use them if I have a blood sugar hypo. It is important to lift out of this low sugar state as soon as possible. Anything that has a high concentration of sugar, like sweets and cordial is effective. I always have some jellies with me or when I'm exercising.

STRESS AND FEAR

I experienced a fair amount of anxiety both with my diabetes and also with my stroke. I believe you need to take each day as it comes and not compound everything by worrying what the future holds. Stress is a big enemy and it is hard to manage. If you have a young family there is always something more important than looking after yourself. Make exercise and caring for yourself one of the priorities. Try not to be afraid—just accept the daily challenges and face them one at a time.

FAMILY

The diabetic diet is good for everyone! If we all lived on a low GI, high protein, low sugar, moderate carb diet with heaps of fresh fruit and vegetables we would all be healthier. So my advice is to include the family in your regime.

DINING OUT

Eating in restaurants creates a challenge for diabetics, mainly because you are not sure about all the ingredients used in the cooking. For example, some Thai food is high in palm sugar and coconut cream, which are both bad for diabetics. Always ask for information, and research the style of food at the restaurant you are visiting. Call in advance if you need something special. Most restaurants will be pleased to prepare something for you if they have notice. If in doubt, stick with simple grilled fish or meat and salad. Most cuisines offer a variation on this simple combination.

YOUR BODY, YOUR LIFE

As a nutritionist, one of the most common requests is for delicious, easy recipes that busy people can prepare while keeping their health goals on track. With at least 60 per cent of adults living in Western countries battling weight, blood sugar and cholesterol issues, this is not always easy.

As powerful influencers over what people eat, chefs, educators, nutritionists and health advisers all have a role to play when it comes to improving health. Clear messages about the role of certain foods in contributing to health risk factors is crucial, as is an understanding of eating behaviour to ensure the advice we give is not only scientifically sound but user-friendly for anyone aiming to maintain work, life and family balance.

The principles of healthy eating are the same—whether or not you're trying to prevent or control diabetes—it is about getting the right mix of the key nutrients. Following this mix, you can easily cook food that your family and friends can enjoy.

In this book, Michael has created a wonderful balance between tasty, yet easy to prepare food with a nutritional profile that ultimately supports weight control and good health long term. His focus is on portion size, carbohydrate balance and nutrient dense ingredient choices.

Perhaps, most appealing is the amazing mix of salads, roasted and grilled foods which contain what I like to call the perfect mix of carbs, proteins and good fats to keep us healthy, our blood sugars regulated but most importantly happy with the foods we are eating.

Fresh fruit and vegetables are so important in our diet and these recipes celebrate these fabulous ingredients. Michael is always looking to increase the fibre content and keep that GI low. You will also find low fat recipes here.

Enjoying good food with friends and family is one of life's most simple pleasures and managing health issues including heart disease and diabetes should not impinge this. Mixing good food with good health does not have to be difficult, it is simply a matter of getting the balance right for the majority of meals that we eat and *Blood Sugar* has managed to achieve this.

Susie Burrell
Nutritionist
B.Nutr & Diet (Hons), B.Sc (Psych)(Hons)

BRUNCH AND LIGHT MEALS

STONE GROUND MUESLI HOT CAKES

These are filling and a much healthier way of eating pancakes.

60g (2oz) self-raising flour

60g (2oz) stone ground whole-wheat flour

¼ teaspoon baking soda/bicarbonate of soda

½ cup whole rolled oats

2 tablespoons slivered almond

1 tablespoon LSA (ground linseeds, sunflower seeds
   and almonds)

1 tablespoon agave syrup

2 eggs

250ml (8fl oz) low-fat milk

cooking spray

VANILLA YOGHURT

1 cup low-fat natural yoghurt

2 tablespoons agave syrup

1 vanilla bean, split lengthways

RASPBERRY CRUSH

1 punnet (150g/5oz) raspberries

1 teaspoon agave syrup

1 Combine flours, baking soda, oats, almonds and LSA in a large bowl and make a well in the centre. In a separate bowl, whisk together the agave, eggs and milk. Pour this into the dry ingredients. Mix until combined. The batter should be the consistency of double cream. Set aside for 30 minutes.

2 Meanwhile, mix yoghurt and agave syrup together. Scrape seeds from vanilla bean and stir into yoghurt. Refrigerate until needed.

3 Place half the raspberries into a bowl with the agave and crush with a fork until broken down. Stir in remaining raspberries and set aside.

4 Heat a non-stick frying pan and spray with cooking spray. Ladle spoonfuls of pancake batter into pan and cook for about 1 minute, or until bubbles appear on the surface of the pancake. Turn over and cook a further 45–60 seconds. Turn onto a plate and repeat with remaining batter.

5 Serve pancakes with raspberry sauce and a spoonful of vanilla yoghurt.

SERVES 4-6

SLOW-BAKED TURKISH DATES AND PEACHES WITH PORRIDGE

2 ripe peaches, halved

4 fresh Turkish dates, seeds removed

1 tablespoon date honey sauce (see Sauces and
  Dressings)

½ cup rolled oats

pinch of salt

625ml (1 pint) low-fat milk

1 tablespoon pumpkin seeds

1 tablespoon sunflower seeds

1 tablespoon linseeds

extra hot milk to serve

1 Preheat oven to 200°C (400°F/gas mark 6).

2 Place peaches and dates into a roasting dish and drizzle over date honey sauce. Roast for 30 minutes or until fruit is soft and the sauce is a syrup. Set aside to cool.

3 Meanwhile, place oats and salt into a medium saucepan and add half the milk, set aside for 5–10 minutes to help soften the oats. Add remaining milk and cook over medium heat until it boils. Reduce heat to low and stir until soft and creamy, approximately 15 minutes.

4 Stir the seeds into the porridge, then serve with warmed peaches and dates and drizzle with extra syrup.

SERVES 4

I love food and life. They are magic when enjoyed together.

BLUEBERRY AND TOFU PROTEIN SHAKE

This is a high protein start to the day, great after a walk or swim.

90g (3oz) silken/soft tofu
½ cup fresh or frozen blueberries
1 banana
1 tablespoon agave syrup
2 tablespoons unprocessed bran
2 egg whites (optional)
3 cups chilled low-fat milk
2 teaspoons chia seeds

1 Combine all ingredients except chia seeds into a blender and pulse until smooth. Stir in the chia seeds then serve immediately in large chilled glasses.

2 Garnish with some berries.

SERVES 4

Chef's note: You can buy chia seeds from health food shops and many supermarkets.

STRAWBERRY, CUCUMBER AND ORANGE COOLER WITH MINT ICE

A cool refreshing drink, to enjoy in moderation.

1 bunch mint, small leaves picked
120ml (4fl oz) cranberry juice
120ml (4fl oz) apple juice
750ml (24fl oz) water
8 strawberries, hulled and sliced
2 large cucumbers
2 oranges sliced
agave syrup to taste
1 lemon, finely sliced

1 Place one mint leaf into each cube of an ice cube tray and cover with water; freeze until completely frozen.

2 Blend juices and water with half of the strawberries, one peeled cucumber and one peeled orange. Strain through a fine sieve to remove excess pulp. Taste and adjust sweetness with the agave syrup. Refrigerate until ready to serve.

3 To serve, finely slice remaining cucumber and orange and place into a large jug with the strawberries, lemon and remaining mint. Add the ice cubes and pour over cooler, stir well and serve

SERVES 4-6

BANANA AND BERRY ICED SMOOTHIE

This is an iced breakfast treat. Use ripe fruit.

3 large ripe bananas, peeled and sliced
juice and zest of ½ lemon
1 tablespoon agave syrup
1 cup non-fat natural yoghurt
1 cup of low-fat milk
1 cup bran
1 punnet (150g/5oz) raspberries

1 Blend bananas with lemon, agave, yoghurt, milk and bran until smooth. Pour into a deep dish. Cover with plastic wrap and freeze until semi-frozen for about 2 hours.

2 To serve, spoon balls of banana mixture and layer in tall glasses. Top with fresh raspberries; serve immediately.

SERVES 4-6

HOMEMADE BAKED BEANS, POACHED EGGS AND HAM

Beans are perfect for protein balance.

2 cups dried haricot beans
olive oil
1 onion, finely chopped
2 cloves of garlic, crushed
2 celery sticks, chopped
1 teaspoon mustard powder
pinch cayenne pepper
2 cups bottled tomato sauce (passata)

2 tablespoons cider vinegar
2 long green chillies, seeds removed and chopped

TO SERVE
poached eggs
toast
ham

1 Cover and soak beans in cold water overnight. Drain, rinse and drain again.

2 Heat oil in a large casserole dish and cook onion, garlic and celery over medium heat until softened. Add remaining ingredients. Add the soaked beans and mix well.

3 Add enough water to cover the beans. Place the lid on and simmer for 2½–3 hours over a low heat, or until beans are tender and sauce has reduced and thickened.

4 Serve beans on the side with poached eggs on toast with ham optional.

SERVES 4

APPLE AND PEAR PASTE

*This is my own alternative to jam. Just a small amount on toast is like a reward to me.
I spread cream cheese on first.*

4 ripe pears
4 red apples
2 tablespoons agave syrup
½ teaspoon vanilla-bean paste
125ml (4fl oz) pear nectar juice

1 Preheat oven to 160°C (320°F/gas mark 2-3).

2 Peel, core and dice pears and apples and place into a large baking dish. Add agave and vanilla paste; pour over nectar.

3 Bake in oven, uncovered, for 1 hour. Stir occasionally while baking.

4 Remove from the oven and place apple and pears into a large saucepan. Mash fruit lightly with the back of a fork, bring to the boil and continue cooking until fruit has reduced and thickened.

5 Spoon into a dish and allow to cool.

6 Place in a jar with a seal-tight lid. This can be kept in the fridge for up to 2 weeks.

MAKES 1 MEDIUM-SIZED JAR

ORANGE MARMALADE

This is not technically marmalade. Enjoy this in small amounts with low-fat ricotta or cream cheese on toast.

3 large oranges, sliced with skin on
30ml (1fl oz) honey
60ml (2fl oz) agave syrup

1 Place oranges into a medium saucepan and add enough water to come half way up the side of the pan. Cover and bring to a simmer. Cook for 10 minutes or until orange slices have softened.

2 Drain and discard any juices. Return orange to the same pan. Add honey and agave and stir to coat.

3 Cook over a very low heat for 1 hour, stirring occasionally. The oranges should begin to fall apart and the marmalade will thicken slightly.

4 Remove and cool. Cover and refrigerate until ready to serve. This can be kept in the fridge for up to two weeks.

MAKES 1 MEDIUM-SIZED JAR

MY SIMPLE FIGS ON TOAST WITH RICOTTA

Replace butter with ricotta for a perfect snack.

4 slices of seeded bread
100g (3½oz) low-fat ricotta
2 ripe black figs (or fresh raspberries or strawberries)
1 teaspoon agave syrup

1 Toast the bread then mash the ricotta onto it using the back of a fork. Slice the figs and also mash them onto the ricotta.

2 Drizzle with a little agave syrup and enjoy with coffee or tea.

SERVES 4

LEMON CHICKEN SCHNITZEL SANDWICH

A sandwich can be a balanced meal.

2 chicken breast fillets

2 thick slices of day-old sourdough bread

2 tablespoons almond meal

2 teaspoons sesame seeds

2 tablespoons pumpkin seeds

2 tablespoons plain flour

1 egg, beaten

vegetable oil for shallow frying

MUSTARD MAYONNAISE

3 teaspoons Dijon mustard

¼ cup low-fat mayonnaise

TO SERVE

fresh sourdough rolls

salad leaves

sliced avocado

sliced tomato

1 Cut each chicken breast in half, slicing through the middle to make two thin fillets. Place between sheets of plastic wrap and pound lightly with a meat mallet to flatten slightly.

2 Remove crust from sourdough and process in a food processor until thin crumbs form. Add almond meal, sesame seeds and pumpkin seeds and pulse 1 to 2 times extra. Tip onto a flat plate or tray.

3 Dust chicken fillets in flour and dip into beaten egg. Crumb in bread/nut mixture. Heat a little oil in a non-stick skillet and cook fillets over medium heat until golden and cooked through. Drain on kitchen towel to absorb excess oil.

4 To make the rolls, mix mayonnaise and mustard together and spread over split rolls. Place avocado and sliced tomato followed by the chicken. Add extra salad to taste.

SERVES 4

HERB ROAST CHICKEN BAGUETTE WITH HAM AND ROASTED TOMATO

Look no butter! But the taste is delicious.

4 Roma tomatoes
salt and freshly ground black pepper
drizzle of extra virgin olive oil
4 whole-wheat baguette rolls, split
1 bunch rocket (arugula)
180g (6oz) cold green herb chicken (see recipe index)
120g (4oz) shaved leg ham

1 Preheat oven to 180°C (350°F/gas mark 4).

2 Halve tomatoes and place cut side up onto a cooking sheet. Season with salt and pepper and drizzle with a small amount of olive oil.

3 Roast in oven for 35–45 minutes. Tomatoes should be soft but still intact. Set aside to cool while building your sandwich.

4 Place rocket on the base of the roll and top with slices of cold chicken, followed by shaved ham. Cut cooled tomato halves in half again and place over the top of sandwich.

SERVES 4-6

SNACKS

FRESH CHILLI NUT MIX

Full of flavour, this is a great snack.

180g (6oz) blanched almonds
180g (6oz) peanuts
180g (6oz) cashew nuts
1 long red chilli, seeds removed and sliced
1 long green chilli, seeds removed and sliced
1 teaspoon smoked paprika powder
drizzle of olive oil
sea salt and freshly ground black pepper
zest of 1 lemon

1 Preheat oven to 180°C (350°F/gas mark 4).

2 Combine nuts, chillies, paprika and olive oil and mix well. Spread out onto a cooking sheet and roast in oven for 30 minutes or until golden and crisp. Turn out onto kitchen paper to absorb any excess oil.

3 Season with a pinch of sea salt, freshly ground black pepper and lemon zest. Serve immediately or store in an airtight container until required.

SERVES 6

ASIAN-STYLE GRILLED TUNA DIP OR WRAP

This dip and sandwich filling is very versatile.

410g (14oz) tuna steaks
cooking spray
¼ cup Thai green curry paste
½ bunch coriander (cilantro) leaves and stem, coarsely
   chopped
¼ cup low-fat mayonnaise
1 teaspoon freshly grated ginger
1 tablespoon fish sauce

1 teaspoon agave syrup
juice of ½ lime
1 long green chilli, seeds removed and finely chopped

TO SERVE
sprinkle of spring onion (scallion), bean sprouts,
   coriander (cilantro)
4-6 soft, low-fat tortilla wraps

1 Lightly spray tuna with cooking spray. Cook in a non-stick skillet (frying pan) over medium heat until cooked through. Remove and cool.

2 Chop tuna and place into the bowl of a food processor along with curry paste, coriander, mayonnaise, ginger, fish sauce, agave and lime juice. Process until smooth. Taste and adjust seasoning if required.

3 Stir through chilli and refrigerate until ready to serve.

4 Serve with crackers as a dip or as a filling for a wrap.

5 TO MAKE A WRAP
For a wrap, smear a good spoonful of tuna dip onto a soft low-fat tortilla and top with sliced scallion, bean sprouts and fresh coriander (optional red chillies to taste). Roll up the wrap and serve immediately.

SERVES 4–6

If you are diabetic, you should accept that you have probably eaten your last potato chip.

SMOKED SALMON AND FRESH HERB MOUSSE

A great pre-dinner nibble.

300g (10oz) cold smoked salmon
zest of 1 lemon
pinch of salt and white pepper
½ bunch dill, leaves picked and chopped
200ml (7fl oz) light cream
60g (2oz) butter, melted
½ bunch each of chervil, chives, parsley, finely chopped
toasted soy and linseed bread, to serve

1 Place salmon, zest, seasoning and dill into the bowl of a food processor and pulse until broken down, but not smooth.

2 Add cream and continue to pulse until salmon is creamy and smooth. Be careful not to overprocess.

3 Spoon into ramekins or dishes and top with melted butter and some mixed fresh herbs. Cover and refrigerate for at least one hour before serving.

4 Serve with toasted soy and linseed bread.

SERVES 6

Chef's note: The melted butter acts as a natural 'lid' to preserve in the fridge. It can be scooped off before serving.

FUNKY MEZZE PLATTER: BABA GANOUSH

3 medium eggplants (aubergines), halved
3 tablespoons extra virgin olive oil
1 clove of garlic
pinch of salt
2 tablespoons lemon juice
1 tablespoons tahini (sesame seed paste)
100g (3½oz) non-fat natural yoghurt

1 Preheat oven to 200°C (400°F/gas mark 6).

2 Brush eggplant with a little of the oil and rub each one with some garlic. Roast in oven for 40–45 minutes or until completely collapsed and soft.

3 When cool enough to handle, scrape out flesh and place into a food processor. Add remaining ingredients and process until smooth.

4 Taste and add more a little more salt or lemon juice if required. Refrigerate until ready to serve.

SERVES 6 AS PART OF A MEZZE PLATTER

FUNKY MEZZE PLATTER: WHITE BEAN DIP

2 cups cooked white beans
1 clove of garlic, chopped
1 bay leaf
2 tablespoons lemon juice
125ml (4fl oz) chicken broth/stock
100g (3½oz) low-fat fetta, crumbled
salt

1 Heat beans with garlic, bay leaf, lemon juice and stock in a saucepan for 10 minutes until soft. Strain and discard liquid. Cool a little before processing until completely smooth.

2 Add fetta and salt and process again until smooth.

3 Taste and add a little more salt or lemon juice if required. Refrigerate until ready to serve.

SERVES 6 AS PART OF A MEZZE PLATTER

FUNKY MEZZE PLATTER: ROAST BEETROOT DIP

470g (1lb) medium-sized beetroot, washed and trimmed

1 tablespoon olive oil

½ bunch fresh thyme

1 tablespoon red wine vinegar

2 tablespoons low-fat natural yoghurt

salt and pepper to taste

100g (3½oz) whole almonds

1 Preheat oven to 180°C (350°F).

2 Place beetroot bulbs into a roasting dish. Rub with olive oil and scatter over thyme leaves. Cover tightly with aluminium foil and roast in oven for 1 hour or until beetroot is soft. Remove and cool completely.

3 Peel and chop roasted beetroot. Place into a food processor with the remaining ingredients. Process until smooth and season to taste. Refrigerate until ready to serve.

SERVES 6 AS PART OF A MEZZE PLATTER

FUNKY MEZZE PLATTER: PARMESAN CHIPS

230g (8oz) parmigiano reggiano (parmesan) cheese

1 Preheat oven to 180°C (350°F/gas mark 4). Line a tray with baking paper.

2 Grate parmesan with a coarse grater. Place tablespoons of grated cheese onto the tray in 5cm (2-inch) circles, leaving enough space in between for each circle to spread. Continue with remaining cheese.

3 Bake for 2–3 minutes or until just melted and lacy. Remove and cool on tray until hardened. Store in an airtight container until ready to serve.

MAKES 12

ZUCCHINI HUMMUS WITH MUSTARD AND TOFU

A really low GI snack or entertainer.

4 large zucchini (courgettes), diced
1 red onion, cut into wedges
1 x 425g (14½oz) can chickpeas, rinsed and drained
2 tablespoons mustard seed oil
salt and freshly ground black pepper
290g (10oz) silken tofu
110ml (3fl oz) vegetable oil
¼ cup tahini (sesame seed paste)
juice of 1 lemon
vegetable sticks or crusty seeded bread, to serve

1 Preheat oven to 180°C (350°F/gas mark 4).

2 Toss zucchini, onion and chickpeas in mustard seed oil and roast in oven for 45 minutes or until vegetables are completely soft. Remove and season with salt and pepper; allow to cool completely.

3 Place into the base of a food processor and process until smooth. Add remaining ingredients and process again until completely smooth. Taste and adjust seasoning with extra lemon juice or salt and pepper. Refrigerate until ready to serve.

4 Serve with fresh cut vegetable sticks or crusty seeded bread.

SERVES 6

SALADS AND VEGETABLES

MY 'HOT' CHICKEN CAESAR SALAD

High in protein, low in carbs, this salad is perfect any time of day.

6 skinless chicken thigh fillets
8 low-fat bacon rashers
2 garlic bulbs
1 tablespoon extra virgin olive oil
freshly ground black pepper
3 thick slices sourdough bread
1 baby cos (romaine) lettuce, washed

DRESSING
3 anchovies, chopped (optional)
zest and juice of 1 lemon
¼ bunch parsley, finely chopped, plus extra for garnish
2 tablespoons extra virgin olive oil
¼ cup light sour cream
2 hardboiled eggs, peeled and coarsely chopped

30g (1oz) parmesan cheese, grated

1 Preheat oven to 230°C (450°F/gas mark 8).

2 Place chicken, bacon and garlic bulbs into a roasting dish. Drizzle over olive oil and season with black pepper. Roast in oven for 25 minutes. Rip up sourdough and add to the roasting dish. Cook for a further 15 minutes. Set aside to cool, then roughly chop cooked chicken and bacon.

3 Squeeze roasted garlic meat from the skin into a pestle and mortar. Pound anchovies, lemon and parsley until thick and smooth. Stir in oil, sour cream and eggs.

4 To serve, rip up lettuce and place into a bowl and top with chicken, bacon and toasted bread. Drizzle over dressing and parsley and sprinkle with parmesan.

SERVES 4-6

SUMMER PEACH SALAD

This is my favourite salad.

4 ripe peaches, halved and stones removed
2 teaspoons low-fat spread or butter, melted
1 teaspoon caster (superfine) sugar

DRESSING
¼ cup low-fat crème fraiche
2 tablespoons unsweetened low-fat natural yoghurt
juice of 1 lemon
¼ bunch mint, finely chopped
pinch sea salt
freshly ground black pepper
1 teaspoon agave syrup

SALAD
1 bunch rocket (arugula)
1 ball buffalo mozzarella
60g (2oz) pine nuts, toasted
½ pomegranate, seeds removed

1 Preheat oven to 200°C (400°F/gas mark 6).

2 Place peaches cut side up into a roasting dish. Brush with a little melted butter and dust with sugar. Roast in oven for 25 minutes or until caramelised. Remove and cool slightly.

3 Mix dressing ingredients together and season with salt and pepper.

4 Place rocket onto a serving platter. Tear the peaches and mozzarella into pieces and scatter over the top. Season with freshly ground black pepper and sea salt.

5 Drizzle over dressing and scatter with pine nuts and pomegranate seeds.

SERVES 4-6

Learn to listen to your body
and treat it with respect.

BBQ PORK SALAD

2 tablespoons soy sauce

1 tablespoon hoisin sauce

1 tablespoon Shaoxing wine (Chinese rice wine)

1 tablespoon honey

2 teaspoons caster (superfine) sugar

1 teaspoon Chinese five spice

900g (2lb) pork leg, skin off

sesame oil, for basting

SALAD

2 large cucumbers

1 long red chilli, seeds removed and sliced

1 medium red onion, finely shaved

2 teaspoons black sesame seeds

2 tablespoons rice wine vinegar

1 Mix together sauces, wine, honey, sugar and spices and rub over pork evenly. Cover and refrigerate overnight.

2 Preheat oven to 180°C (350°F/gas mark 4).

3 Place pork onto a rack fitted into a large roasting dish and add a little water to the base. Roast in oven for 1½ hours, turning roast every 30 minutes. Brush pork with sesame oil. Remove from oven and allow to cool.

4 Using your fingers, pull the meat apart into shreds and reserve.

5 To make the salad, slice cucumbers into thin ribbons using a potato peeler and combine with chilli, shaved red onion, sesame seeds and pork. Dress with rice wine vinegar.

SERVES 6

POWER FOOD SALAD

A fantastic source of protein! I often add low-fat fetta to this salad.

1 x 150g (5oz) can chickpeas

1 x 150g (5oz) can 3-bean mix

1 large red onion, finely diced

1 green apple

2 large celery sticks

2 carrots

juice and zest of ½ lemon

6 egg whites

1 cucumber, diced

1 cup fresh podded peas

½ bunch dill, leaves picked

180g (6oz) hot smoked salmon, flaked

1 tablespoon each pumpkin and sunflower seeds

2 tablespoons olive oil

low-fat fetta cheese to garnish (optional)

1 Rinse and drain chickpeas and mixed beans. Place into a bowl with finely chopped red onion.
Using a juicer, juice apple, 1 celery stick and 1 carrot. Mix with lemon juice and zest. Pour this juice over chickpea, bean and onion mix, cover and refrigerate overnight.

2 Lightly beat egg whites and pour into a large hot non-stick skillet (frying pan). Cook a few minutes each side, then turn the omelette out onto a board and roll up. Allow to cool and slice finely.

3 Drain the chickpeas and bean mixture. Place into a large bowl, retaining the liquid. Add 1 diced cucumber and 1 diced carrot with all remaining ingredients.

4 Whisk half of the reserved liquid with olive oil and drizzle over the salad to serve. Crumble fetta over the top if desired.

SERVES 4

Chef's note: Hot smoked salmon is available in most good supermarkets and delicatessens. Alternatively, you can use fresh cooked salmon or trout.

SPINACH, PEA AND FETTA SALAD

160g (6oz) soft low-fat fetta
1 lemon
freshly ground black pepper
2 tablespoons extra virgin olive oil
160g (6oz) baby spinach leaves
60g (2oz) fresh peas (out of the pod)
1 bunch mint, coarsely chopped

1 Combine fetta, zest of the lemon, pepper and olive oil in a bowl; cover and refrigerate overnight.

2 To serve, place spinach leaves into a serving bowl. Add peas, mint and fetta mixture.

3 Dice the flesh of half the lemon and mix through.

4 Drizzle the olive oil from the fetta over the top and season with black pepper to taste.

SERVES 6

BAKED FIG AND HAZELNUT SALAD

An end of summer treat.

8 ripe figs (black or green)

150g (10oz) low-fat ricotta

60g (2oz) blue cheese

2 tablespoons ground hazelnuts

pinch of sea salt and pepper

30ml (1oz) agave syrup

1 teaspoon hazelnut oil

½ cup whole hazelnuts

mixed salad leaves, to serve

1 Preheat oven to 180°C (350°F/gas mark 4).

2 Cut a cross into the top of each fig and squeeze between fingers to open. In a bowl, mix ricotta, blue cheese, agave syrup and ground hazelnut together to form a thick paste; season with salt and pepper.

3 Spoon ricotta mix into the centre of each fig and place into roasting dish just large enough to fit tightly. Drizzle over agave and hazelnut oil and roast for 20 minutes. Scatter over whole hazelnuts and roast for a further 15 minutes.

4 Serve warm with mixed leaf salad, spooning over some of the pan juices.

SERVES 4

ROASTED VEGETABLE SALAD AND LIME DRESSING

Serve this at room temperature.

2 small parsnips, peeled and halved

2 carrots, peeled and halved

470g (1lb) pumpkin, peeled and cut into wedges

470g (1lb) sweet potatoes, peeled and cut in thick slices

2 red capsicum (peppers), seeds removed and cut into
    thick strips

1 celeriac, peeled and cut into wedges

30ml (1fl oz) extra virgin olive oil

½ bunch flat parsley (or chervil, dill or chives)

DRESSING

2 tablespoons white wine

60ml (2fl oz) olive oil

juice of 1 lime

sea salt and freshly ground black pepper

1 Preheat oven to 200°C (400°F/gas mark 6).

2 Toss vegetables with oil and season with salt and pepper. Place into a large roasting dish and bake for 40–45 minutes in oven. Remove and cool slightly. Toss through chopped herbs.

3 Whisk dressing ingredients together and season with salt and pepper; drizzle over salad and serve.

SERVES 6

Chef's note: You can also include or substitute roast beetroot, roast eggplant (aubergine) or roast onion.

SCOTCH BEEF FILLET
AND CARAMELISED ONION SALAD

900g (2lb) beef scotch fillet
splash of extra virgin olive oil
sea salt and freshly ground black pepper
8 small pickling onions, peeled and halved

DRESSING
½ bunch parsley, chopped
2 cloves of garlic, crushed
2 shallots (eschallots), finely chopped
3 tablespoons red wine vinegar
2 tablespoons vegetable oil
1 bunch watercress, leaves picked

1 Preheat oven to 200°C (400°F/gas mark 6).

2 Brush beef lightly with oil and season with salt and pepper. Seal on a preheated non-stick skillet until brown and caramelised on all sides.

3 Place into a roasting dish, along with onions, and roast for 45 minutes. Remove beef and rest for 20 minutes.

4 Return onions to oven and cook until completely soft and falling apart. Allow onions to cool and flake to separate the layers.

5 Mix dressing ingredients together and toss through onions, picked watercress and any pan juices.

6 Slice beef thinly and lay onto a serving platter. Top with onion and watercress salad and serve immediately.

SERVES 6

BAKED RICOTTA, PEAR, CELERY AND WALNUT SALAD

A light meal that satisfies and is low in fat.

600g (20oz) low-fat ricotta
1 egg
½ bunch mint, finely chopped
½ bunch marjoram, finely chopped
zest and juice of 1 lemon
sea salt and freshly ground black pepper
2 pears, halved
cooking spray

¼ cup light cream
½ bunch celery, thinly sliced
½ cup walnuts, coarsely chopped

1 Preheat oven to 200°C (400°F/gas mark 6).

2 In a bowl, mix ricotta thoroughly until smooth. Add egg, herbs and lemon zest. Season with salt and pepper.

3 Place into a greased baking dish and cook in oven for 25 minutes. Remove and allow to cool. Keep the oven on.

4 Spray 1 pear with cooking spray and grill or roast in a oven until soft and caramelised. Slice the other pear thinly.

5 Mix cream with juice of half the lemon. Season with salt and pepper. Add celery and fresh pear to the cream mixture and serve with baked ricotta and grilled pears. Sprinkle with walnuts to serve.

SERVES 6

SALAD CAPRESE: FRESH BASIL, TOMATO AND MOZZARELLA SALAD

This simple salad is so low in GI.

2 punnets (250g) cherry or vine ripened tomatoes, halved
1 bunch basil
4 balls, each 90g (3oz) buffalo mozzarella, sliced
drizzle of extra virgin olive oil
freshly ground black pepper

1 Place tomatoes, basil and mozzarella onto individual serving plates and drizzle a little olive oil over the top. Finish with a twist of freshly ground black pepper.

SERVES 4

SOUPS

ASIAN-STYLE PRAWN BROTH WITH BUCKWHEAT NOODLES

Buckwheat is a healthy, low GI noodle.

16 jumbo raw king prawns (shrimp)
1.25 litres (2 pints) chicken stock
1 small piece of fresh ginger, sliced
1 stick of lemongrass, trimmed
2 small red chillies, sliced
3 kaffir lime leaves
150g (5oz) broccoli, cut into small florets
180g (6oz) mushrooms, sliced

1 tablespoon fish sauce
juice of 1 lime
pinch of sugar
120g (4oz) buckwheat noodles, cooked
1 bunch coriander (cilantro)

1 Peel the prawns, leaving their tails on.

2 Place heads and shell trimmings into a large pan with stock and ginger slices. Lightly bash lemongrass with the back of a knife and add to the pan, along with chillies and kaffir lime leaves.

3 Bring to the simmer and cook for 15 minutes, or until fragrant and prawns have changed colour. Strain and keep the broth only.

4 Put vegetables into a small pan. Cover with the hot broth and simmer for 2 minutes. Add the prawn tails and cook for a further 2 minutes until prawns are firm and pink.

5 Stir in fish sauce, lime juice and sugar to taste.

6 Place cooked noodles into serving bowls. Add fresh coriander and divide the prawns and vegetables between the bowls. Pour the hot broth over and serve.

SERVES 4-6

THICK AND GREEN PRIMAVERA MINESTRONE

This soup fills you up and has no fat and no sugar.

410g (14oz) asparagus, trimmed
1 white onion, diced
1 clove of garlic, finely chopped
1 tablespoon extra virgin olive oil
2.5 litres (4 pints) vegetable stock
sea salt and white pepper
2 sticks of celery, diced
1 large zucchini (courgette), diced
½ cup fresh peas
¼ cup orzo pasta
2 cups baby spinach leaves

1 Cut the tips off asparagus and reserve. Coarsely chop the stalk and add to a pan with onion, garlic and oil. Cook for 10 minutes until soft but not coloured.

2 Add stock and simmer for 30 minutes. Season to taste.

3 Puree with a stick blender until smooth and return to saucepan. Add celery, zucchini and peas and heat for a few minutes, or until vegetables are just cooked.

4 Meanwhile, cook orzo in boiling water until tender; drain and add to soup. Remove from heat and stir in baby spinach just before serving.

SERVES 4

I always prefer to eat a small amount of something good, rather than a pile of rubbish I know is bad for me.

SPICY SWEET POTATO AND PUMPKIN SOUP

A winter warmer.

800g (1lb 13oz) sweet potato, peeled
490g (17oz) pumpkin, peeled
1 tablespoon harissa paste
2 teaspoons ground cumin
1 clove of garlic, crushed
2 tablespoons extra virgin olive oil
600ml (20fl oz) vegetable stock
1 cup low-fat unsweetened yoghurt
sea salt and freshly ground black pepper

TO SERVE
fresh chives, chopped
red chilli, sliced

1 Preheat oven to 180°C (350°F/gas mark 4).

2 Cut sweet potato and pumpkin into large dice. Place into a bowl with harissa, cumin, garlic and oil. Toss to coat evenly and roast in a tray in oven for 50 minutes, or until cooked and tender. Transfer into a large pan and cover with stock. Bring to the boil and simmer for 30 minutes.

3 Puree with a stick blender until smooth. Blend in yoghurt.

4 Adjust seasoning to taste with a little salt and freshly ground black pepper.

5 Serve hot soup topped with chopped chives and a slice of red chilli.

SERVES 6

CORN AND CRAB SOUP

I love the lightness of this soup.

2 fresh corn cobs
1 clove of garlic, sliced
1 bay leaf
1 teaspoon vegetable oil
3 spring onions (scallions), finely sliced
180g (6oz) cooked crabmeat
2 egg whites
sea salt and white pepper
1 litre (2 pints) vegetable stock

1 Cut kernels off cobs and set aside. Place cob, husks, garlic and bay leaf into a large saucepan with 1 litre (2 pints) of vegetable stock; bring to the boil. Reduce heat and simmer for 45 minutes.

2 Heat vegetable oil in a second pan. Cook the corn kernels and scallions for 15 minutes, or until softened. Strain the hot stock over the corn and bring back to the simmer. Cook for 15 minutes.

3 Add the crabmeat and stir through lightly whisked egg whites until egg ribbons form. Season to taste. Serve topped with finely chopped spring onions.

SERVES 4-6

ROMESCO SOUP WITH CHICKEN AND CHORIZO SAUSAGE

4 chicken drumsticks, skin removed
freshly ground black pepper
4 red capsicums (peppers)
½ chorizo sausage
2 shallots (eschallots), finely chopped
2 cloves of garlic, finely chopped
1 teaspoon smoked paprika

1.25 litres (2 pints) chicken stock
2 tablespoons almond meal
2 tablespoons red wine vinegar

1 Preheat oven to 180°C (350°F/gas mark 4). Place chicken in a roasting dish and season with black pepper. Roast for 45 minutes.

2 Meanwhile, place capsicum onto a tray and roast alongside chicken until skin blisters and they become soft. Remove chicken and capsicum from the oven. Cover capsicum with a tea towel and allow to cool completely before peeling and removing seeds.

3 Warm a saucepan and cook diced chorizo, shallots and garlic together in a little oil for a few minutes.. Stir in paprika and cook for a further minute. Add chicken stock, red wine vinegar and peeled peppers. Cover and simmer for 30 minutes. Remove chorizo with a slotted spoon and reserve for garnish.

4 Remove from the heat and stir in almond meal. Puree with a stick blender until smooth. Bring back to the simmer.

5 Shred the chicken and mix with chorizo. Ladle hot soup into bowls and top with chicken, chorizo and freshly ground black pepper.

SERVES 4-6

SLOW-COOKED OSSO BUCCO SOUP

Easy to freeze in portions and warm up when you need a boost.

2 osso bucco bones (cut on the bone from butcher)

1 tablespoon extra virgin olive oil

1 onion, finely diced

1 carrot, finely diced

1 stick of celery, finely diced

1 leek, washed and trimmed

1 bay leaf

1 sprig of thyme

splash of white wine

2 cups bottled tomato sauce (passata)

1 litre (2 pints) beef stock (broth)

1 cup dried borlotti beans, soaked overnight

GREMOLATA

¼ bunch parsley, finely chopped

zest of 1 lemon

freshly ground black pepper

1 In a hot saucepan, brown osso bucco in a little oil for 2 minutes each side. Add onion, vegetables and bay leaf. Add white wine, tomato passata and the beef stock. Bring to the boil. Add beans and cover with a lid. Simmer for 1½ hours, or until meat falls from the bone.

2 Remove bones from liquid and flake meat with a fork. Check consistency; if soup is too thick add a little more stock or water.

3 To serve, spoon meat into the centre of plate and pour over soup. Garnish with gremolata of parsley, lemon and freshly ground black pepper.

SERVES 4-6

GAZPACHO 'MARRAKESH'

A low-fat chilled soup for summer.

1 teaspoon fennel seeds
1 teaspoon cumin seeds
1 teaspoon coriander seeds
2 large cucumbers, chopped (including skin and seeds)
900g (2lb) ripe tomatoes, chopped (including skin and seeds)
1 red onion chopped roughly
2 long green chillies, seeded and chopped
sea salt and black pepper
110ml (3fl oz) red wine vinegar

½ clove of garlic, grated
zest of 1 lemon
fresh parsley and mint, to serve

1 Heat the whole spices in a small non-stick skillet (frying pan) for a few minutes until they are fragrant. Transfer to a mortar and pestle and grind up to a powder.

2 In a bowl, place chopped cucumber, diced tomato, red onion and chilli; mix through roasted ground spices and a little salt. Add red wine vinegar and cover with film. Refrigerate for at least 3 hours, preferably overnight.

3 Using a blender, process until smooth. Add a little grated garlic and season with salt and pepper to taste. Serve soup chilled with a squeeze of lemon juice and chopped fresh herbs.

SERVES 4-6

PASTA, RICE AND EGGS

ANGELA'S VEGGIE LASAGNE

Cut out the meat and cut down on the fat.

290g (10oz) pumpkin, peeled and sliced

6 large plum tomatoes, halved

1 tablespoon extra virgin olive oil

½ bunch thyme, leaves picked and chopped

cooking spray

12 dried lasagne sheets

210g (7oz) low-fat ricotta

210g (7oz) low-fat fetta

½ bunch sage, leaves picked and chopped

TO SERVE

zest of 1 lemon

2 tablespoons pumpkin seeds

1 Preheat oven to 180°C (350°F).

2 Place pumpkin and tomatoes into a roasting tray, sprinkle with thyme leaves and pepper, drizzle over oil. Roast in oven for 25–30 minutes, or until soft. Remove and cool slightly.

3 Grease a small lasagne dish and line the base with sheets of lasagne to fit. (You may need to break some in half.)

4 Spoon over half of the cooked pumpkin and tomato and crumble over a third of the ricotta, fetta and chopped herbs. Repeat with a second layer of lasagne sheets, pumpkin and tomato, cheese and herbs.

5 To finish, top lasagne with remaining pasta sheets and sprinkle over remaining cheese, herbs, lemon zest and pumpkin seeds. Roast in oven for 45–50 minutes. Serve with Spinach Salad (see recipe index).

SERVES 4

ANGEL HAIR PASTA WITH SALMON AND CHILLI LIME DRESSING

4 x 180g (6oz) salmon fillet, skin on
sea salt
3 tablespoons olive oil
zest and juice of 2 limes
1 tablespoon agave syrup
1 long red chilli, seeds removed and finely shredded
2 kaffir lime leaves, finely shredded
80g (3oz) angel hair pasta

1 Rub both sides of salmon fillets with a little sea salt and some olive oil. Cook in a heated non-stick skillet for 1–2 minutes each side, leaving salmon rare.

2 Meanwhile, mix lime zest, juice, agave, chilli and kaffir lime leaves together, then whisk in the remaining olive oil.

3 Cook pasta in a large pan of boiling salted water until al dente. Drain well and rinse under cold water. Drain again, place into a bowl and mix through the chilli and lime dressing.

4 Spoon pasta onto plates and serve with salmon.

SERVES 4

OLIVE OIL EGGS WITH ASPARAGUS, CHEESE AND JAMON

A great alternative for breakfast.

1 tablespoon olive oil
½ cup olives, sliced with stones removed
4 large eggs
2 bunches asparagus, trimmed
90g (3oz) jamón, serrano or prosciutto (Spanish or Italian
    air-dried ham)
freshly ground sea salt and black pepper
120g (4oz) manchego cheese, shaved (or other hard
    sheep's milk cheese)

1 Warm oil and some of the olives in a non-stick skillet (frying pan) for 3 minutes. Carefully crack in eggs. Cook on a gentle heat until eggs are just cooked.

2 Cook asparagus in a pan of boiling salted water until just tender; drain and place on serving plate.

3 To serve, place the cooked eggs on top of the asparagus; place the ham around and scatter more of the olives over. Season with sea salt and black pepper. Top with shaved cheese.

4 Serve with some seeded crusty bread.

SERVES 4

BAKED EGG AND BACON PIES WITH PARMESAN

8 sheets filo (phyllo) pastry
cooking spray
100g (3½oz) low-fat bacon, diced
1 cup baby spinach leaves, chopped
4 eggs
60g (2oz) parmesan, grated
freshly ground black pepper

1 Preheat oven to 180°C (350°F/gas mark 4).

2 Cut each sheet of filo into four squares and lightly coat with cooking spray. Stack the four squares roughly on top of each other and place into the holes of a greased muffin tin or into individual ramekins.

3 In a small fry pan, fry the bacon for 4 minutes, then add the spinach. Season and allow to cool.

4 Divide spinach and bacon evenly between each dish and crack an egg over the top. Sprinkle with parmesan and black pepper.

5 Bake in oven for 10–15 minutes, or until pastry is golden and egg has just set.

SERVES 4

Low fat bacon is best.

PAELLA FRIED RICE

6 chicken wings

1 tablespoon olive oil

2 cloves of garlic, finely chopped

1 onion, finely chopped

1 cup fresh peas

1 cup of low GI or brown rice

1 teaspoon smoked paprika

⅓ cup tomato puree

8 medium raw prawns (shrimps), peeled

8 mussels

sea salt, to taste

chopped parsley, to garnish

1 Brown chicken wings in hot oil in a large non-stick skillet (frying pan) until golden and cooked. Add garlic, onion, peas and rice to the hot pan and cook for 3 minutes. Stir in paprika and tomato puree and mix well.

2 Add prawns (shrimps) and mussels to the same pan. Cook for 3 minutes, making sure mussels open and prawns (shrimps) cook.

3 Turn up to heat to high and add the cooked rice.

4 Season to taste with salt and serve hot, topped with chopped parsley.

SERVES 6

'ONE POT' CHICKEN AND RICE

A simple family dish.

2 tablespoons olive oil

4 chicken Marylands, skin removed

salt and freshly ground black pepper

1 onion, sliced

2 cloves of garlic, crushed

2 celery sticks, sliced

1 red capsicum (pepper), cut into strips

1 yellow capsicum (pepper), cut into strips

1 x 425g (14½oz) can red kidney beans, drained

1 cup low GI or brown rice

sprig of fresh thyme

3 cups chicken or vegetable stock

1 Preheat oven to 200°C (400°F/gas mark 6).

2 Warm oil in a non-stick skillet (frying pan). Season chicken with salt and pepper and sear until golden brown, but not cooked through. Remove and set aside.

3 Add onion, garlic, celery and capsicum to the same pan and cook for 5 minutes. Tip into a large, deep roasting dish, along with beans and rice. Mix well and smooth out into an even layer.

4 Place chicken and thyme over the top of rice and pour in hot stock; cover with a lid or aluminium foil. Roast in oven for 25 minutes.

5 Serve chicken on the bone with the rice or pull the chicken meat from the bone and mix through the rice.

6 Adjust the seasoning to taste.

SERVES 4

MUSHROOM, PEA AND BOCCONCINI OMELETTE

A fantastic source of protein!

1 tablespoon olive oil
1 clove of garlic, crushed
120g (4oz) mushrooms, quartered
90g (3oz) fresh peas
3 egg whites, lightly beaten
2 egg yolks, lightly beaten
sea salt and freshly ground black pepper
4 baby bocconcini balls

1 Heat oil in a small non-stick skillet (frying pan) and cook garlic and mushrooms for 2-3 minutes. Add peas and cook for a further 2 minutes.

2 Carefully fold beaten egg whites and yolks together. Season with salt and pepper. Pour over mushrooms and peas and allow to set for 15 seconds on the bottom of the pan.

3 Drop bocconcini over the top and place directly under a hot grill (broiler) for 2 minutes, or until puffed up and cooked through.

4 Serve wedges with crusty sourdough or linseed bread.

SERVES 4

OPEN CANNELLONI WITH PORK MEATBALLS

My twist on a lasagne.

485g (1lb 1oz) ground pork mince meat
1 clove of garlic, crushed
½ small red onion, finely chopped
1 teaspoon crushed black peppercorns
sea salt
1 egg white
350g (½lb) fresh egg lasagne sheets
300mls Napolitana sauce (see Sauces and Dressings)
60g (2oz) grated parmesan

1 Preheat moderate oven to 180°C (350°F/gas mark 4). Mix ground meat with garlic, onion, black pepper, salt and egg white in a bowl. Dip your hands in cold water. Roll mixture into 14 even meatballs and set aside.

2 Grease a large baking dish and spoon Napolitana sauce on the base.

3 Trim lasagne sheets into squares and place a meatball into the centre of each one. Place into baking dish; repeat with remaining lasagne and meatballs.

4 Pour over remaining Napolitano sauce to cover and sprinkle with parmesan. Bake in oven for 45–50 minutes.

SERVES 6

SEAFOOD

ROASTED SALMON AND BABY NIÇOISE SALAD

Impressive and healthy! Perfect!

720g (24oz) salmon fillet, skin on and pin boned
splash of extra virgin olive oil
salt and pepper, to taste

DRESSING
1 teaspoon Dijon mustard
2 tablespoons sherry vinegar
90ml (3fl oz) extra virgin olive oil
1 egg white (optional)

SALAD
150g (5oz) small potatoes, cooked and halved
150g (5oz) baby green beans, cooked and chilled
130g (4oz) cherry or grape tomatoes, halved and roasted
60g (2oz) black olives
3 hard-boiled eggs, peeled and quartered
½ bunch basil, leaves picked

1 Preheat oven to 180°C (350°F/gas mark 4).

2 Place salmon fillet, skin side down, onto a lined baking sheet. Brush with a little olive oil and season with salt and pepper. Bake for 7 minutes.

3 Meanwhile, whisk mustard, vinegar and oil together with egg white. Season and adjust consistency with water.

4 Place potatoes, green beans, tomatoes, olives and boiled eggs in a bowl with the basil leaves. Season and mix together.

5 To serve, spoon the salad onto the salmon fillet and drizzle with the dressing.

SERVES 4-6

SEAFOOD PIE WITH CRISP POTATOES

350g (12oz) sea bass fillet

350g (12oz) salmon fillet, skin off

350g (12oz) peeled medium green prawns (shrimps)

8 oysters

8 scallops

120g (4oz) butter, melted

30g (1oz) plain all-purpose flour

splash of white wine (optional)

1 litre (2 pints) fish stock

salt and white pepper

1 large potato

1 Preheat oven to 200°C (400°F/gas mark 6).

2 Cut fish fillets into large 1-inch (2.5cm) cubes and toss with remaining seafood. Place into the base of a shallow ceramic baking dish.

3 Melt a quarter of the butter in a saucepan and stir in flour; cook for a few minutes before adding wine. Cook until all the wine has evaporated. Slowly add the stock, stirring continuously, until sauce comes to the boil and thickens. Season with a little salt and pepper and cool slightly before pouring over seafood.

4 Finely slice potato into thin matchsticks and toss with remaining melted butter. Pile loosely over seafood and sauce so that potatoes extend above the rim of the baking dish. Bake in oven for 30 minutes or until potatoes are cooked, crisp and golden.

5 Serve seafood pie with a crisp green salad.

SERVES 6

GRILLED TUNA WITH TOFU AND SOY

High in omega 3 and low in fat–perfect.

470g (1lb) firm silken tofu

2 tablespoons white miso paste

1 teaspoon caster (superfine) sugar

3 tablespoons light soy sauce

2 tablespoons rice wine vinegar

2 teaspoons sesame oil

4 x 180g (6oz) tuna fillet steaks

cooking spray

400g (14oz) baby spinach leaves, washed

toasted sesame seeds, for garnish

1 Place tofu onto a plate that is small enough to fit into a steamer. Combine miso, sugar, soy, vinegar and sesame oil together and spoon most of the mixture over tofu. Steam in a steamer for 10 minutes or until tender.

2 Spray tuna fillets with cooking spray and cook on a lightly greased non-stick skillet (frying pan) for 1–2 minutes each side, leaving undercooked.

3 In a small pan of boiling salted water, wilt the spinach until collapsed. Drain well.

4 To serve, spoon warm tofu onto the tuna steak with the spinach. Drizzle over remaining soy and miso dressing and sprinkle with toasted sesame seeds.

SERVES 4

FENNEL SALT SWORDFISH AND RUBY GRAPEFRUIT SALAD

I love this texture—crispy and fresh.

FENNEL SALT
2 tablespoons sea salt
zest of 1 lemon
½ bunch dill, leaves picked and chopped
1 teaspoon fennel seeds

4 x 180g (6oz) swordfish, tuna or kingfish fillets
splash of extra virgin olive oil

SALAD
½ bunch celery
1 large ruby grapefruit, peeled
1 sprig dill or fennel tips
2 tablespoons extra virgin olive oil

1 Preheat oven to 180°C (350°F).

2 Pound salt, lemon zest, dill and fennel seeds in a mortar and pestle. Place mix onto a tray in oven for 15 minutes or until dried out. Cool slightly before pounding again to make a fine salt.

3 Brush fish with a little oil; sprinkle with the fennel salt.

4 Peel, trim and finely slice celery. Add some of the leaves from the celery heart and toss into a bowl. Segment grapefruit and add to celery with the juice. Add dill or fennel tips and mix; pour in remaining olive oil.

5 Sear swordfish on a hot barbeque grill for 1-2 minutes each side. Serve with salad.

SERVES 4

WARM SEAFOOD AND QUINOA SALAD

Quinoa is a new supergrain which is high in protein.

1 cup quinoa
240g (8oz) sea bass fillet
240g (8oz) salmon fillet, skin off
240g (8oz) peeled medium raw prawns (shrimps)
150g (5oz) scallops
splash of extra virgin olive oil
salt and pepper

DRESSING
1 large clove of garlic, finely grated
2 sprigs rosemary, leaves picked and finely chopped
2–3 anchovy fillets, finely chopped
100ml (23/4fl oz) extra virgin olive oil
zest and juice of 1 lemon
salt and pepper

100g (3½oz) green beans, blanched and refreshed in
  cold water
1 x 25g (4oz) can of red kidney beans, rinsed and drained

1 Rinse quinoa several times in cold water and drain. Cook in a saucepan of boiling salted water for 15 minutes. Drain and rinse again. Set aside.

2 Place seafood onto a baking tray and brush with a little oil. Season with salt and pepper. Grill (broil) 4-8 minutes or until seafood is just cooked.

3 In a mortar and pestle, pound together garlic, rosemary and anchovy fillets until broken down. Add the oil, lemon zest and juice mix well and adjust the seasoning to taste.

4 Stir dressing into the quinoa, green and kidney beans. Spoon the salad over the warm seafood to serve.

SERVES 4

PUMPKIN-CRUSTED FISH ON MASH

4 x 160g (5oz) sea bass fillets (or equivalent firm flesh
   fish)
1 medium-sized pumpkin, peeled and cut into cubes
1 orange, quartered with peel left on
sea salt and pepper
1 cup non-fat natural yoghurt
¼ bunch basil, leaves picked and shredded
½ cup raw pumpkin seeds
cooking spray

1 Preheat oven to 180°C (350°F/gas mark 4).

2 Place pumpkin and orange into a roasting dish and roast in the oven for 45 minutes, or until pumpkin is cooked. Remove half of the oranges and set aside.

3 Squeeze removed orange segments into the pumpkin and mash coarsely with a fork. Season with salt and pepper and set aside to keep warm.

4 Squeeze juice from remaining orange segments into yoghurt and stir in basil. Season to taste.

5 Crush pumpkin seeds in a mortar and pestle until they have the consistency of coarse breadcrumbs.

6 Season the fish and press each fillet into the pumpkin seeds, ensuring it is evenly covered. Spray lightly with cooking spray and cook in a non-stick skillet (frying pan) for 2–3 minutes each side.

7 Serve the fish on the warm pumpkin mash with a spoon of the orange and basil yoghurt.

SERVES 4

SNAPPER CEVICHE WITH LIME AND HERBS

290g (10oz) fresh snapper or white fish fillets, all bones
    removed
1 shallot (scallion), finely chopped
½ cup, approx 100g (3½oz) fennel, trimmed and finely
    chopped
1 medium red chilli, seeded and finely chopped
zest and juice of 1 lime
zest and juice of 1 lemon
2 tablespoons olive oil
¼ bunch chervil, leaves picked and finely chopped

¼ bunch chives, finely chopped
sea salt and pepper

1 Place snapper fillet into the freezer for 15 minutes until firm but not frozen.

2 Using a sharp knife, slice the snapper as thinly as possible and place neatly onto serving plates (this is the ceviche).

3 In a small bowl, mix together shallots, fennel and red chilli. Add half grated zest and juice of the lime and lemon, stir in the oil and season heavily with salt and pepper. Allow this to stand for at least 1 hour .

4 Adjust the seasoning and acid taste with remaining juice.

5 To serve, add the fresh herbs to the dressing and spoon a small amount over each plate of fish

6 Serve remaining dressing in a bowl on the side, garnish with some fresh salad leaves

SERVES 6

Chef's note: This is a simple fresh-tasting ceviche. Do not leave dressing on fish for long or it will dominate the flavour of the fresh fish.

FISH BURGER WITH LENTIL DIP AND CUCUMBER YOGHURT

High in fibre and protein–a great combination.

470g (1lb) firm white fish fillets (bass, snapper, monkfish), boned and skinless
2 egg whites
½ bunch coriander (cilantro), chopped
1 teaspoon harissa paste
pinch of salt

MOROCCAN LENTIL DIP
1 tablespoon olive oil
1 clove of garlic, crushed
1 teaspoon ground cumin seeds
1 teaspoon ground coriander seeds

pinch of ground fennel seeds
1 x 400g (14oz) can brown lentils, rinsed and drained
1 teaspoon brown sugar

CUCUMBER YOGHURT
1 small cucumber, grated
1 cup non-fat natural yoghurt
juice of 1 lemon
¼ bunch mint, leaves picked and finely chopped

TO SERVE
wholemeal soy and linseed rolls and mixed leaves

1 Chill the fish and egg whites in the freezer for 15 minutes.

2 Using a blender process fish and harissa paste together until smooth. Add the egg whites and season with salt and pepper. Add the coriander (cilantro) and mix well. Divide mixture into 8 small patties and coat with cooking spray. Cook in a hot non-stick skillet (frying pan) for 3 minutes each side or until cooked, golden and firm to touch.

3 To make the Moroccan dip, cook garlic in oil for 1–2 minutes and stir in spices. Heat for a further 1 minute and add lentils, sugar and ¼ cup of water. Simmer for 10 minutes or until liquid has evaporated and lentils are thick. Cool slightly and process until smooth. Season with salt to taste and set aside.

4 Grate cucumber and squeeze out excess liquid; stir into yoghurt along with lemon juice and mint.

5 To serve, place one slice of bread onto serving plates and top with 2 fish patties. Serve with a dollop of lentil dip and cucumber yoghurt and mixed leaves.

SERVES 4

POACHED FISH FILLET WITH BROCCOLINI

2 cups low-fat milk
½ red onion, cut into rings
1 bay leaf
6 whole black peppercorns
pinch of sea salt
12 small carrots, trimmed
4 baby potatoes, cooked
4 x 160g (5oz) firm white fish fillet (skin off)
steamed broccolini to serve

1 Place milk, onion, bay leaf, peppercorns and salt into a large deep non-stick skillet (frying pan) and bring to the simmer over low heat.

2 Add carrots and potatoes and cook for 20 minutes. Add the fish and continue cooking for a further 3 minutes. Until fish is just firm to the touch.

3 To serve, using a slotted spoon, remove fish and vegetables from milk and arrange on plates. Serve with steamed broccolini and a little of the cooking liquid.

SERVES 4

Chef's note: This is a gentle way of cooking fish and creates a wonderful soft sweetness to the dish.

STEAMED BLACK PEPPER MUSSELS

An easy meal or a starter to share.

1 tablespoon olive oil

2 cloves of garlic, finely chopped

1 bay leaf

1 medium green chilli, seeds removed and chopped

2 spring onions (scallions), sliced

freshly ground black pepper

900g (2lb) mussels, cleaned

splash of white wine (optional)

2 tablespoons light cream

1 bunch coriander (cilantro), leaves picked and roughly chopped

1 bunch parsley, leaves picked and roughly chopped

1 Heat oil in a large pan or wok and cook garlic, bay leaf chilli, spring onions and black pepper for a few minutes or until fragrant.

2 Add the mussels and a splash of white wine. Cover with lid and cook for 2 minutes. Shake pan and continue cooking until mussels open.

3 Stir through cream, coriander and parsley.

4 Serve hot from the pot immediately with some crusty seeded bread.

SERVES 4

MEAT

GRILLED LAMB WITH PEARS, POMEGRANATE AND SUMAC

1 teaspoon sumac spice

zest of 1 lemon

2 pears, cut in quarters

1 x 120g (4oz) can of vine leaves, drained and rinsed

1 cinnamon quill

1 piece of preserved lemon, rinsed and skin finely
    chopped

1 cup non-fat natural yoghurt

12 French-trimmed lamb cutlets

seeds from ½ pomegranate

1 Preheat oven to 150°C (300°F).

2 Rub a good pinch of sumac and lemon zest over pears. Wrap each in a vine leaf.

3 Place in a roasting dish with cinnamon quill and cook in oven for 45 minutes.

4 Mix together preserved lemon, yoghurt and a little pinch of sumac; set aside.

5 Grill (broil) lamb cutlets for 2 minutes each side, or until cooked to your liking.

6 To serve, unwrap pears and discard cinnamon. Place onto plates with lamb cutlets.
Serve with a dollop of yoghurt and sprinkle over pomegranate seeds.

SERVES 4

Chef's note: French-trimmed bones are scraped clean. Ask your butcher to prepare them or you can do it yourself with a sharp knife.

LAMB SPIEDINI, WITH FETTA, BABA GANOUSH AND TOMATOES

A fantastic source of protein cooked on the barbecue or grill.

BLACK PEPPER FETTA
290g (10oz) low-fat fetta
1 tablespoon freshly crushed black pepper
2 tablespoons extra virgin olive oil

12 fresh rosemary sticks
470g (1lb) lamb leg, cut into 2.5-cm (1-inch) cubes
1 onion, cut into large dice
12 small mushrooms
12 small fresh bay leaves
cooking spray
sea salt and freshly ground black pepper
2 stems truss cherry tomatoes
baba ganoush, to serve (see recipe index)

1 To make the black pepper fetta, season fetta with freshly ground black pepper and drizzle with olive oil. Cover and refrigerate until required.

2 Thread rosemary sticks alternatively with lamb, onion and whole baby mushrooms. Finish with a bay leaf. Spray lightly with cooking spray and season with salt and pepper.

3 Cook on a preheated barbeque plate (grill) for a few minutes, turning regularly, until meat is cooked and browned. Remove and set aside to keep warm.

4 Season tomato and spray with cooking spray. Place onto a preheated barbeque plate (grill) and cook 2–3 minutes, or until tomato has softened.

5 Serve skewers with fetta, roasted tomatoes and a dollop of baba ganoush.

SERVES 6

SLOW-BRAISED LAMB SHANKS
AND HERBED BROWN RICE

2 tablespoons olive oil

4 small lamb shanks, French-trimmed

6 small onions, peeled

2 cloves of garlic, chopped

2 celery sticks, thickly sliced

3 carrots, peeled and halved

6 small leeks

1 cup red wine

625ml (1 pint) tomato sauce (passata)

2 cups cooked brown rice

½ bunch each of oregano, marjoram, thyme, leaves
    picked and finely chopped

1 Heat oil in a large casserole dish and brown lamb shanks in batches. Remove lamb and add vegetables, cook for a few minutes. Stir in wine and cook until wine has reduced by half.

2 Add tomato passata and return lamb to pan. Add enough water so that the shanks are just covered and bring to the boil. Reduce heat, cover with lid and simmer for 1½ hours or until sauce is thick and lamb is tender.

3 Remove lamb from casserole and coarsely chop cooked vegetables.

4 Warm rice in boiling water or in a microwave.

5 Mix rice with the vegetables and sauce from lamb. Stir fresh herbs through.

6 Serve tomato and herbed rice with lamb shanks.

SERVES 4

Chef's note: French-trimmed bones are scraped clean. Ask your butcher to prepare them or you can do it yourself with a sharp knife.

GREEN ROAST HERB AND LEMON CHICKEN

1 x 1kg (2¼lb) fresh chicken
1 bunch fresh parsley
1 lemon juice and zest
2 tablespoons capers
2 anchovies
1/3 cup (100 ml) olive oil
sea salt and pepper

1 Place all ingredients except chicken into a blender and pulse to a paste.

2 Put the chicken into a baking dish, season with salt and pepper and rub the green paste well into the chicken, on and under the skin. Refrigerate and leave for 1 hour.

3 Preheat oven to 180°C (360°F/gas mark 4).

4 Roast in oven for 50 minutes until cooked.

5 Remove and carve into portions. Serve with vegetables or salad, or allow to cool for cold sandwiches.

SERVES 4-6

Chef's note: You can remove the skin on the plate and the flavours remain in the chicken.

Everyone will be on your case about what you eat. You must be prepared to be honest with yourself.

GARLIC CHICKEN STEAK WITH ANTIPASTO

Skinless chicken means low fat

ANTIPASTO DRESSING

½ cup semi-dried tomatoes, finely chopped

1 red onion, finely chopped

zest and juice of 1 lemon

2 tablespoons baby capers, finely chopped

½ cup mixed pitted olives, finely sliced

½ bunch parsley, finely chopped

2 tablespoons extra virgin olive oil

4 skinless chicken breast fillets

cooking spray

2 cloves of garlic, crushed

30g (1oz) butter

salad leaves, to serve

1 Combine antipasto ingredients together in a large bowl. Add 2 tablespoons of the oil and mix well.

2 Cut each chicken breast in half, slicing through the middle to make two thin fillets. Place between sheets of plastic wrap and pound lightly with a meat mallet to flatten into thin steaks.

3 Spray with cooking spray and cook in a hot non-stick skillet (frying pan) with the garlic and butter for 2 minutes each side.

4 Place directly onto serving plate. Spoon over the dressing and serve with salad leaves.

SERVES 4

CRISPY BUTTERMILK AND NUT CHICKEN MARYLAND

625ml (16fl oz) buttermilk
2 teaspoons garlic powder
pinch of cayenne pepper
1 teaspoon paprika
pinch of ground white pepper
1 teaspoon ground coriander seeds
4 chicken Maryland pieces, skin removed
1 cup dried panko breadcrumbs
½ cup almond meal

cooking spray
fresh lemon, to serve
reduced fat mayonnaise, to serve
   (see Sauces and Dressings)
salad leaves, to serve

1 Mix buttermilk, garlic powder, cayenne, paprika and pepper with coriander seeds. Pour over chicken. Cover and marinate overnight.

2 Preheat oven to 200°C (400°F/gas mark 6).

3 Combine panko crumbs with almond meal and mix well.

4 Coat drained chicken evenly in the crumb mix and place onto a lined flat baking sheet. Spray lightly with cooking spray and bake in oven for 50–60 minutes, turning chicken over halfway through the cooking time. Chicken should be cooked through with a golden and crisp crumb. Season with sea salt.

5 Serve hot with fresh lemon, reduced fat mayo and salad leaves.

SERVES 4–6

Chef's note: Panko breadcrumbs are Japanese-style crumbs and are lighter. They can be substituted with conventional breadcrumbs.

GRILLED SIRLOIN STEAK
WITH ROASTED MUSHROOM PATÉ

MUSHROOM PATE
470g (1lb) mixed mushrooms, roughly chopped
1 shallot, finely chopped
1 clove of garlic, crushed
1 sprig thyme, leaves picked and chopped
sea salt and freshly ground black pepper
¼ cup thick sour cream

4 x 180g (6oz) sirloin steaks
cooking spray

1 Cook mushrooms in a non-stick skillet (frying pan) over high heat for 5 minutes. Add eschalot, garlic and thyme leaves and cook until mushrooms have cooked and all liquid has evaporated.

2 Season with salt and pepper and cool completely. Transfer to a food processor and add sour cream; process until smooth. Form paté into a log and wrap tightly with plastic wrap. Chill until completely hardened.

3 Lightly spray steaks with cooking spray and season with salt and pepper. Cook on hot grill for 2 minutes each side or until cooked to your liking.

4 Slice mushroom paté into 2.5cm (1-inch) thick slices and serve melting over hot steak.

SERVES 4

POLENTA-CRUSTED PORK
WITH FENNEL AND ORANGE SALAD

4 pork cutlets, trimmed of extra fat

1 cup coarse polenta

cooking spray

1 large fennel bulb, trimmed

2 oranges, peeled and segmented

½ bunch flat-leaf parsley, leaves picked

sea salt and pepper

2 tablespoons date honey sauce (see Sauces
    and Dressings)

1 Press pork cutlets into the polenta to coat evenly. Spray cutlets with cooking spray and cook in a non-stick skillet (frying pan) over medium high heat until cooked through. Remove and rest for 5 minutes.

2 Shave fennel on a cutter into very thin slices. Mix with orange segments and any juices. Add picked parsley.

3 Mix date honey sauce roughly and toss through salad. Season with salt and pepper.

4 Serve cutlets with salad.

SERVES 4

SMOKED PAPRIKA PORK WITH SPANISH-STYLE RICE

SPANISH-STYLE RICE
4 large vine-ripened tomatoes
1 tablespoon olive oil
1 onion
½ red capsicum (pepper), seeds removed and diced
splash of white wine
pinch of saffron
1 cup low GI or brown rice
500ml (16fl oz) vegetable stock

sea salt and pepper
2 teaspoons smoked paprika
2 tablespoons olive oil
pinch of salt
2 medium-sized pork fillets, trimmed of all sinew

1 Preheat oven to 180°C (350°F/gas mark 4).

2 Cut tops off tomatoes and scoop out tomato flesh, leaving tomato hollow but intact. Coarsely chop tomato flesh and set aside.

3 Heat oil in a non-stick skillet (frying pan) and cook onion and peppers for 2–3 minutes or until softened. Add tomato flesh, wine and saffron and cook for a further 5 minutes.

4 Stir in rice and stock and season with salt and pepper. Simmer for 15 minutes until rice is just cooked and stock has been absorbed.

5 Spoon rice evenly into tomatoes and bake in oven for 15 minutes.

6 Meanwhile, combine paprika, oil and salt and rub over pork fillet. Pan fry in a non-stick pan for 8 minutes or until cooked.

7 Serve sliced pork with stuffed tomatoes.

SERVES 4

SLOW COOKED TURKEY WITH RICOTTA AND SPINACH

Keeps the top breast meat nice and moist!

120g (4oz) spinach leaves
180g (6oz) low-fat ricotta
1 clove of garlic, crushed
salt and pepper
1 tablespoon olive oil
3kg (10lb) whole turkey
juice and zest of 1 lemon

1 Preheat oven to 150°C (300°F/gas mark 2).

2 Blanch spinach in boiling salted water for 1 minute and refresh under cold water. Squeeze as dry as possible. Roughly chop spinach.

3 Mix ricotta in a bowl until smooth. Add the spinach, lemon juice and zest, garlic and season with salt and pepper.

4 Force your fingers between the skin and breast meat. Spoon the ricotta mix into this area, spreading out evenly. Rub the turkey with a little olive oil.

5 Roast in a deep roasting pan in oven for 2 hours Remove and rest for 15 minutes in a warm place before carving.

6 Serve sliced turkey with roasted vegetable salad (see recipe index)

SERVES 6-8

CRUSTED BEEF WITH STICKY SWEET POTATO AND MUSTARD CREAM

One of my favourite Sunday lunches.

STICKY SWEET POTATO
700g (1lb 9oz) sweet potato
1 tablespoon agave syrup
2 tablespoons light soy sauce

480g (16oz) beef tenderloin
cooking spray
90g (3oz) sunflower seeds
90g (3oz) whole almonds
90g (3oz) walnuts

60g (2oz) low-fat spread or butter

MUSTARD AND HORSERADISH CREAM
2 tablespoons horseradish puree or sauce
2 tablespoons wholegrain mustard
1 clove of garlic, crushed
1 shallot, finely chopped
¼ bunch parsley, finely chopped
90g (3oz) light sour cream
sea salt and freshly ground black pepper

1 Preheat oven to 200°C (400°F/gas mark 6).

2 Peel and cut sweet potato into large chunks. Coat well with agave and soy sauce and place onto a shallow baking sheet. Roast in oven for 35 minutes, turning over halfway through the cooking time.

3 Spray tenderloin with cooking spray and seal evenly in a hot non-stick skillet (frying pan) for 2 minutes each side, or until brown. Remove and cool.

4 Process seeds and nuts to a coarse crumb. Add butter and process until just mixed through. Press nut crust onto beef tenderloin and reduce heat to a moderate oven (180°C/350°F) and bake for 25 minutes. Set aside to rest for 10 minutes before slicing.

5 Mix mustard and horseradish ingredients together and season to taste.

6 Serve sliced beef with sweet potato and mustard and horseradish cream.

SERVES 6

DESSERTS

POACHED PEARS IN A BAG WITH NUT AND SEED CRUNCH COOKIES

These cookies are a treat on their own.

NUT AND SEED CRUNCH COOKIES

½ cup almonds, chopped

½ cup walnuts, chopped

½ cup LSA (linseeds, sunflower seeds and almonds)

2 tablespoons sunflower seeds

2 tablespoons honey, warmed

2 egg whites, beaten

POACHED PEARS

625ml (20fl oz) pear juice or concentrate

120g (4oz) agave syrup

1 vanilla bean, split into four

4 pears, peeled and cored

1 lemon zest

sugar-free ice cream, to serve

1 Preheat oven to 180°C (350°F/gas mark 4).

2 Place nuts in food processor and pulse until broken down into a rough crumb. Add LSA and sunflower seeds. Stir in honey and eggs and mix well.

3 Place teaspoon-sized mounds onto a greased tray. Bake for 20 minutes or until golden. Allow to cool on a wire rack.

4 In a saucepan, heat pear juice, agave syrup and vanilla bean. Drop in the pears and cover with a lid. Simmer on low heat for 20 minutes or until pears are soft and cooked. Carefully remove from the liquid.

5 Cut 4 large squares of parchment paper and place a pear into the centre of each one. Add a piece of the vanilla bean and a tablespoonful of the liquid with a slice of lemon zest. Enclose and seal by tying with twine. Bake in a moderate (180°C/350°F) oven for 12 minutes.

6 To serve, place the bags on each plate with a little of the pear cooking liquid on the side and some of the nut and seed crunch. Split the bags at the table and serve with some sugar-free ice cream.

SERVES 4

ALMOND AND STRAWBERRY MILK JELLY WITH BERRY AND LYCHEE SALAD

4 sheets of gelatine
½ punnet (approx 125g) strawberries, hulled and sliced
1¾ cup almond milk
60g (2oz) agave syrup
½ cup whipping cream

BERRY AND LYCHEE SALAD
1 punnet strawberries, halved
1 punnet raspberries, halved
6 lychees, peeled and halved

1 Soak gelatine in cold water.

2 Place strawberries and ¼ cup of the milk into a blender and puree until smooth. Strain through a fine sieve and discard solids. Set aside strawberry milk.

3 Heat remaining milk and agave together until it comes to the boil. Add blended strawberry milk and mix well.

4 Squeeze excess water from gelatine and stir in hot milk until completely dissolved.
Cool before stirring in whipped cream.

5 Pour into 6 light dariole (jelly) moulds and refrigerate until set.

6 To serve, dip the bottom of each mould into hot water and invert onto plates. Serve with berries and lychees.

SERVES 6

BAKED CHOC 'N' NUT RICOTTA CHEESECAKES

NUT BASE
¼ cup chopped walnuts
¼ cup slivered almonds
¼ cup chopped hazelnuts
½ cup almond meal
1 tablespoon melted butter
1 tablespoon agave syrup
1 egg white, lightly beaten

FILLING
900g (2lb) low-fat ricotta cheese
½ cup non-fat natural yoghurt
60g (2oz) agave syrup
zest of 1 lemon
2 tablespoons cornflour
2 eggs, lightly beaten
1 cup very dark chocolate buttons
icing sugar and berries to serve

1 Preheat oven to 150°C (300°F/gas mark 2).

2 Process nuts in a food processor until they have the texture of breadcrumbs. Melt butter with agave syrup and pour into nut mix. Add egg white and mix well with a spoon.

3 Line the base of 6 greased 6-cm (2-inch) rings with greaseproof paper. Spoon in and bake the nutbase in oven for 15 minutes. Remove and allow to cool in the tins (see next page).

4 Beat ricotta in a bowl with electric beaters until smooth. Stir in yoghurt, agave syrup, lemon, cornflour and eggs. Beat until completely mixed.

5 Fold through chocolate buttons and pour into prepared tins. Increase heat to 180°C (350°F/gas mark 4) and bake for 20 minutes.

6 Remove from the oven and allow to cool. Remove from the tins and place onto serving platter.

7 Dust with a little icing sugar. Serve sliced with fresh berries.

SERVES 6–8

WARM CHERRY CUSTARD PIE WITH ROASTED CHERRY SAUCE

You can swap cherries for strawberries.

ROASTED CHERRIES
290g (10oz) fresh black cherries
1 tablespoon maple syrup

210g (7oz) light cream cheese, softened
290g (10oz) low-fat ricotta
1 whole egg
2 teaspoons vanilla essence
8 sheets filo (phyllo) pastry
cooking spray
¼ cup slivered almonds

1 Preheat oven to 180°C (350°F).

2 Toss cherries in maple syrup and roast for 10 minutes. Remove and cover until completely cool. Strain and reserve syrup.

3 Beat cream cheese and ricotta together until creamy and smooth. Add eggs and vanilla and mix well.

4 Spray each sheet of filo pastry with cooking spray and stack together. Push pastry into a loaf pan or terrine mould, ensuring there is an overhang on each side. Pour ricotta mixture into the centre. Scatter roasted cherries over the top and fold over pastry sides to enclose. Sprinkle over almonds and bake in oven for 30 minutes.

5 Warm the reserved cherry syrup and serve with slices of the cherry pie.

SERVES 6

BAKED FIG AND ALMOND CUSTARD

6 large ripe figs, halved lengthways
500ml (16fl oz) low-fat milk
90g (3oz) almond meal
3 eggs, beaten
30g (1oz) agave syrup
pinch of salt

2 tablespoons slivered almonds
honey, for drizzling

1 Arrange figs, cut side up, in a large greased pie dish and set aside.

2 Place milk and almond meal into a saucepan and warm gently for 5 minutes. Remove and stand for 5 minutes.

3 Beat eggs, agave and salt together until well combined and stir in cooled milk. Pour carefully over figs and sprinkle with slivered almonds.

4 Bake for 35–40 minutes in a moderate oven (180°C/350°F) or until just set. Remove and serve warm, drizzled with honey.

SERVES 6

PASSIONFRUIT YOGHURT POTS WITH CHOCOLATE BISCOTTI

These flavours work so together.

CHOCOLATE BISCOTTI

2 eggs

1 egg yolk

1 cup caster (superfine) sugar or equivalent sugar substitute

2 teaspoons vanilla essence

1 cup almond meal

1 cup plain (all-purpose) flour

2 tablespoons unsweetened cocoa powder

¾ teaspoon baking powder

¼ teaspoon baking soda (bicarbonate of soda)

YOGURT POTS

2 gelatine leaves (soaked in water)

½ cup passionfruit pulp

2 tablespoons agave syrup

¼ bunch mint, leaves picked and finely chopped

500ml (16fl oz) non-fat natural yoghurt

fresh passionfruit and mint, to serve

1 Preheat oven to 180°C (350°F/gas mark 4).

2 Beat eggs, yolk, sugar and vanilla extract in a bowl with electric beaters until thick and pale yellow. Sift dry ingredients together and fold into egg mix.

3 Turn onto a floured surface and knead lightly to form a dough. Roll into a 20-cm (8-inch) log. Press the top with your hand and place onto a lined baking sheet.

4 Bake for 15–20 minutes. Remove and allow to cool.

5 Using a sharp knife, cut biscotti an angle into 1-cm (½-inch) thick slices. Return to oven and bake for a further 10 minutes until crisp. Cool on a wire rack.

continued

6 Strain passionfruit through a sieve and collect juice in a saucepan. Discard half the seeds and pulp and return the rest to the juice.

7 Stir in agave and heat gently until it just comes to the boil. Remove from heat.
Squeeze excess water from gelatine and stir into hot syrup until gelatine dissolves. Allow to cool.

8 Stir passionfruit syrup and mint into yoghurt and mix well. Spoon into 6 glasses.

9 Serve with chocolate biscotti, fresh passionfruit and mint.

SERVES 6

BAKED CHOCOLATE AND ORANGE PUDDING

This is really quick to make. Everyone loves this one!

600ml (20fl oz) low-fat milk
zest of 1 orange
1 teaspoon vanilla extract
90g (3oz) agave syrup
2 tablespoons cocoa powder, sifted
2 eggs
2 tablespoons butter
3 thick slices seeded brown bread
cocoa and icing sugar, for dusting
sugar-free ice cream, to serve

1 Preheat oven to 180°C (350°F/gas mark 4).

2 Bring milk to the boil in a saucepan with orange zest, vanilla and agave syrup. Remove from heat and cool slightly.

3 Mix cocoa to a paste in a cup with a spoon of cold milk, then whisk into the hot milk. Lightly whisk the eggs in a bowl. Pour the hot milk mixture over the top (ensure the milk is not boiling). Continue to stir.

4 Spread butter onto the slices of bread and arrange in a small baking dish. Pour the chocolate custard mixture evenly over the top. Allow to stand for 15 mins to allow bread to absorb custard.

5 Bake in oven for 35 minutes. Dust with a little cocoa and icing sugar. Serve warm with some light or sugar-free ice cream.

SERVES 6

BAKED ORANGE AND PEANUT DELICIOUS

2 oranges
2 egg yolks
60g (2oz) caster (superfine) sugar
½ cup non-fat dry milk powder
2 tablespoons self-raising flour
120g (4oz) peanuts, ground
4 egg whites
cooking spray

1 Preheat oven to 180°C (350°F/gas mark 4).

2 Zest oranges and squeeze 180ml (6fl oz) of juice from the flesh. Mix zest and juice with egg yolks, ¼ cup water, half the sugar, milk powder, flour and peanuts until well combined.

3 In a separate bowl, whisk egg whites until soft peaks form. Add remaining sugar and continue whisking until thick and glossy. Fold egg whites into orange juice mixture.

4 Pour into a baking dish of approximately 1 litre (2 pints) capacity, greased with cooking spray. Place into a larger roasting pan and pour in enough hot water to come halfway up the sides of the dish. Bake for 35–40 minutes.

5 Sprinkle with a little icing sugar and serve immediately.

SERVES 6

A VERY DARK CHOCOLATE MOUSSE
WITH BANANAS

This is a once-a-year treat. Use very good chocolate!

230g (8oz) dark chocolate (70% cocoa)

1 tablespoon butter

2 egg yolks

30g (1oz) agave syrup

200ml (8fl oz) heavy whipping cream (thickened cream)

1 teaspoon vanilla bean paste

60g (2oz) chopped walnuts

60g (2oz) chopped hazelnuts

60g (2oz chopped almonds

4 bananas, peeled and halved lengthways

caster (superfine) sugar

2 tablespoons roasted hazelnuts

icing sugar, to dust

1 Melt chocolate and butter in a double boiler over a saucepan of simmering water. Stir and allow to cool to room temperature.

2 Whisk egg yolks with agave syrup until light and creamy and fold into the chocolate.

3 Meanwhile, whisk cream with vanilla paste until thick.

4 Carefully fold the cream and chopped nuts into the chocolate and egg mix, taking care not to overmix. Pour chocolate mousse into a small dish and chill in the fridge until set.

5 Dust bananas with a little caster sugar and place under a very hot grill to caramelise.

6 To serve, place the caramelised bananas on a plate. With a hot tablespoon, scoop a neat ball or two of the chocolate mousse around the plate. Serve with some crushed, roasted hazelnuts and a light dusting of icing sugar.

SERVES 4–6

Chef's note: This is a real treat! You must only have a small amount! You can also swap the bananas for figs or strawberries to reduce the carbohydrates.

ROAST PEACHES WITH ZABAGLIONE AND SUNFLOWER SEEDS

Late summer peaches are best.

4 peaches or nectarines, stoned and halved
2 tablespoons sunflower seeds
1 tablespoon agave syrup
2 eggs, plus 2 yolks
60ml (2fl oz) peach nectar juice
icing sugar, to dust

1 Preheat oven to 180°C (350°F/gas mark 4).

2 Place peaches, cut side up, into a roasting dish and dust lightly with icing sugar. Sprinkle sunflower seeds on the top and bake in oven for 20 minutes.

3 To make the zabaglione, whisk agave, eggs and yolks together in a bowl over a pan of simmering water, while gradually adding the nectar. Continue to whisk until the mixture is thick, frothy and pale yellow in colour; do not let it get too hot.

4 Serve warm peaches in a small bowl or glass drizzled with zabaglione.

SERVES 4

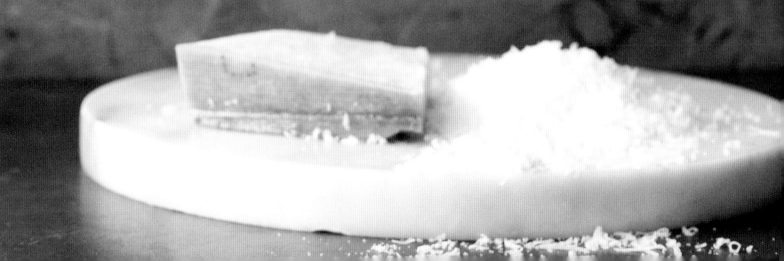

SAUCES AND DRESSINGS

RAW TOMATO AND BASIL SAUCE

1.4kg (3lb) ripe tomatoes
1 clove of garlic, grated finely
pinch of salt and freshly ground black pepper
¼ bunch basil, leaves picked and finely shredded
2 tablespoons extra virgin olive oil

1 With a coarse cheese grater, grate tomatoes into a large bowl with grated garlic, salt and pepper, basil and olive oil. Cover and refrigerate until required.

2 Mix sauce through hot cooked pasta.

MAKES APPROX 1 LITRE (2 PINTS)

NAPOLITANA SAUCE

2 tablespoons olive oil
1 onion finely diced
1kg (2¼lb) ripe tomatoes, roughly chopped
1 clove of garlic crushed
½ bunch basil, chopped
sea salt and pepper

1 Warm a saucepan and add the olive oil. Fry the chopped onion and garlic for 3 minutes until fragrant.

2 Add the chopped tomatoes and cook at a simmer for 45 minutes until thick.

3 Adjust seasoning with salt and pepper.

4 Before serving, stir in the basil leaves. (Photograph right shows sauce before fresh basil is added.)

SERVES 6

CAESAR DRESSING

1 large egg

1 tablespoon lemon juice

1 tablespoon white wine vinegar

1 clove of garlic, crushed

2 teaspoons Dijon mustard

2 anchovies, finely chopped

125ml (4fl oz) non-fat natural yoghurt

½ bunch parsley, chopped

40g (1½oz) parmesan cheese, finely grated

pinch of sea salt

1 Cook egg in boiling water for 3 minutes. Remove and crack open.

2 Spoon semi-cooked egg a bowl. Add lemon juice, vinegar, garlic, mustard and anchovies. grind with mortar and pestle or pulse in blender until well combined.

3 Spoon in yoghurt, a little at a time, until thick and well incorporated. Add parsley and parmesan, adjust seasoning and mix well. Spoon into a clean jar; seal and refrigerate for up to one week.

BASIL AND WALNUT PESTO

2 bunches fresh basil leaves

½ cup walnut halves

2 tablespoons grated parmesan cheese

1 tablespoon red wine vinegar

180ml (6fl oz) olive oil

sea salt and black pepper

1 Place the walnuts and basil leaves into a mortar and pestle or blender with a pinch of sea salt. Grind to a coarse paste and gradually add the olive oil. Combine together to form a thick sauce

2 Season with fresh black pepper and stir in the red wine vinegar to finish.

ASIAN VINAIGRETTE

Dress fish and salads with this fragrant dressing.

1 clove of garlic, crushed
2 teaspoons grated fresh ginger
pinch of salt
juice and zest of 1 lime
3 tablespoons rice wine vinegar
2 tablespoons light soy sauce
2 tablespoons peanut oil
1 tablespoon sesame oil

1 Whisk ingredients together and season to taste with salt and pepper. Alternatively, place into a screw top jar and shake just before using.

2 Refrigerate until required for up to two weeks.

MAKES 6 SERVES

THREE-CITRUS DRESSING

Fresh, light and great on your favourite salad leaves.

juice of 1 lemon
juice of 1 lime
juice of ½ orange
1 tablespoon white wine vinegar
1 teaspoon Dijon mustard
pinch of sugar
60ml (2fl oz) extra virgin olive oil
pinch of sea salt and freshly ground black pepper

1 Whisk ingredients together and season to taste with salt and pepper. Alternatively, place into a screw top jar and shake just before using.

2 Refrigerate until required for up to two weeks.

MAKES 6 SERVES

DATE HONEY SAUCE

I only ever use a little of this at a time.

8 dates, pitted and chopped
juice of ½ lemon
125ml (4fl oz) water
60ml (2fl oz) agave syrup

1 Mash dates lightly with a fork. Place into a small saucepan with lemon juice, water and agave.

2 Cook, stirring over low heat, until the water has been absorbed and it has a thick consistency. Cool completely and store in the refrigerator in a sealed jar.

MAKES 1/3 CUP

WHOLE-EGG, LOW-FAT MAYONNAISE

1 egg
3 egg whites
2 teaspoons Dijon mustard
juice of ½ lemon
2 teaspoons white wine vinegar
pinch of sea salt
180ml (6fl oz) vegetable oil (canola or sunflower)
180ml (6fl oz) non-fat natural yoghurt

1 Whisk eggs, mustard, lemon juice, vinegar and salt together until well combined. Whisking continuously, drizzle in oil a little at a time until completely incorporated.

2 Stir in yoghurt in the same manner until mayonnaise is thick. Taste and adjust seasoning.

3 Spoon into a jar and seal; refrigerate until required for up to one week.

MAKES 6 SERVES

LIGHT CHEESE SAUCE

Great for cauliflower or lasagne.

625ml (20fl oz) low-fat milk
1 small dried bay leaf
1 tablespoon low-fat spread/margarine
1 tablespoon plain (all-purpose) flour
1 teaspoon Dijon mustard
2 tablespoons grated low-fat cheddar cheese
2 tablespoons grated parmesan cheese
freshly ground white pepper

1 Warm milk and bay leaf together until hot. Remove bay leaf and set aside.

2 Melt spread in medium saucepan and stir in flour to form a paste (roux). Cook for 2 minutes. Gradually stir in a third of the milk and cook until it thickens and boils.

3 Gradually add the rest of the milk and continue to cook until sauce comes to the boil and thickens. Whisk out any lumps.

4 Slowly simmer, covered with a lid, for 45 minutes. Remove from the heat. Add mustard and cheeses and stir until melted. Season to taste with white pepper.

MAKES 6 SERVES

BUTTERMILK RANCH-STYLE DRESSING

1 clove of garlic, chopped
pinch of sea salt
½ teaspoon mustard powder
2 tablespoons finely chopped dill
180ml (6fl oz) buttermilk

60ml (2fl oz) low-fat sour cream
2 tablespoons low-fat mayonnaise
juice of ½ lemon
pinch of ground white pepper

1 Combine garlic with a pinch of salt and mash with a fork to finely mince. Mix with remaining ingredients.

2 Spoon into a jar and refrigerate until required for up to one week.

MAKES 6 SERVES

CARAMELISED BALSAMICO DRESSING

2 tablespoons honey
250ml (8fl oz) balsamic vinegar
125ml (4fl oz) water
60ml (2fl oz) extra virgin olive oil
pinch of salt and freshly ground black pepper

1 Mix honey, balsamic vinegar and water together in a small saucepan and bring to a simmer. Reduce by half and allow to cool.

2 Whisk in oil and season with salt and pepper. Pour into a screw-top jar and refrigerate for up to one week. Shake dressing just before using.

MAKES 6 SERVES

WEIGHTS AND MEASURES

SPOONS

Metric sizes are used in this book:

¼ teaspoon	1.25ml
½ metric teaspoon	2.5ml
1 metric teaspoon	5ml
2 teaspoons	10ml
1 tablespoon	20ml

(Note: Australian size is used for tablespoon measurement. Imperial (US) and NZ tablespoon is 15ml)

CUPS

All measures are based on level cupfuls.

LIQUID

1 cup	250ml (9fl oz)
½ cup	125ml (4fl oz)

SOLIDS

1 cup flour	120g (4oz)
1 cup white sugar	180g (6oz)
1 cup light brown sugar	120g (4oz)
1 cup caster sugar	120g (4oz)
1 cup chopped nuts	180g (6oz)
1 cup grated cheese	90g (3oz)

OVEN TEMPERATURES

100°C	very slow	200°F	Gas Mark 1
120°C	very slow	250°F	Gas Mark 1
150°C	slow	300°F	Gas Mark 2
160°C	warm	325°F	Gas Mark 2–3
180°C	moderate	350°F	Gas Mark 4
190°C	moderately hot	375°F	Gas Mark 5
200°C	moderately hot	400°F	Gas Mark 6
220°C	hot	420°F	Gas Mark 7
230°C	very hot	450°F	Gas Mark 8
250°C	very hot	485°F	Gas Mark 9

First published in Australia in 2011 by New Holland Publishers (Australia) Pty Ltd Sydney • Auckland • London • Cape Town

1/66 Gibbes Street Chatswood NSW 2067 Australia 218 Lake Road Northcote Auckland New Zealand
86 Edgware Road London W2 2EA United Kingdom 80 McKenzie Street Cape Town 8001 South Africa

National Library of Australia Cataloguing-in-Publication entry:
    Moore, Michael.
    Blood sugar : inspiring recipes for anyone facing the challenge of diabetes and maintaining good health / Michael Moore.
    ISBN: 9781742571546 (hbk.)
    Includes index.
    Subjects: Diabetes--Diet therapy--Recipes. Cooking (Natural foods)
    641.56314

Publisher: Fiona Schultz
Publishing Manager: Lliane Clarke Designer: Celeste Vlok Photographs: Steve Brown Food stylist: Kathy McKinnon
Production Manager: Olga Dementiev Printed by: Toppan Leefung Printing Limited (China)

10 9 8 7 6 5 4 3 2

Our thanks to: Dinosaur Designs and Mud Australia for the provision of fine crockery and materials for this book.

Although every effort has been made to verify the accuracy of the information contained in this book, it must not be treated as a substitute for medical or professional opinion or advice. Neither the author nor the publishers can be held responsible for any loss, injury or inconvenience sustained by any person arising out of the use, or misuse, of the suggestions, or the failure to take medical care.

ACKNOWLEDGEMENTS

Angela, thank you for your endless love, strength, wisdom and unwavering support. We can continue this journey and embrace the future, together forever.

Eloise, my no 1 girl, you are truly a special gift to me in fact the most perfect gift.

Charlie, my adorable son, please keep being happy and just try to be the best you can.

Mum, Dad, Lisa, Kay, Tom, Sam, Jan and Kirsten—thanks for your love and support and for always being there for us.

My loyal friends—a heartfelt thanks to all of you. Angela couldn't have coped without your amazing love and support. Matt Moran, thanks for bringing me great food in hospital. Trevelyan Bale, my good mate, this is an extra special mention just for you!

To all of my golfing mates at NSW—thank you for your friendship, sense of humour and money!

My medical team (and there's a few of you)—thank you to Rafi Sahagian my GP for keeping a close eye on me; the doctors and nursing staff at Royal North Shore Hospital Stroke Unit, particularly Sam McGuiness who gave me hope that if I did as I was told, I could get on top of this. Thank you cardiologist, Dr Raj Subiah, endocrinologist, Dr Jerry Greenfield, and his assistant Jo.

Paramedics, thank you for being there quickly and getting me to hospital. You are under-resourced, overworked but totally admired.

The Vision team, especially Michael Dunn my trainer, thank you for pushing me to get fitter. It's a complicated job, but together we'll get there!

To the amazing people who helped bring *Blood Sugar* together thank you.

The team at New Holland Publishers: Fiona Schultz—for believing in me and giving me this opportunity to tell my story; Lliane Clarke for your collaboration and project management, Celeste Vlok for your design.

Steve Brown you are an amazing talent with the lense. I am so glad you found your calling.

Kathy McKinnon thank you for your simple and elegant styling.

Brett Luckens thank you for all your work in helping me bring these recipes to life.

Michelle Lucia thanks for interpreting my ideas.

My restaurant team—thank you for growing with me and keeping the business running smoothly

Steven McArthur—thank you for your endless commitment in getting another book on the shelf. I couldn't have done this without your dedication, patience and loyalty. You really are a true friend and confidant.

...and finally Peggy thank you for bringing calmness, light and love into our home.

About the author

Michael Moore is an experienced and respected chef, starting out in some of London's best restaurants. Now 26 years into a career spanning two continents, Michael has owned and managed numerous top restaurants in both London and Sydney including The Ritz Hotel London, Kables, Craigend, Hotel Nikko, The Bluebird London, Bennelong, Prunier's, Bonne Femme and Wildfire.

Michael has earned critical appraise on both sides of the globe, as well as a number of coveted media awards. Michael has appeared on television for the last seven years and is currently the chef and owner of the iconic Summit restaurant and bar in Sydney. *Blood Sugar* is Michael's second book, and follows *Moore to Food*.

www. michaelmoorechef.com
www.summitrestaurant.com.au

INDEX